Becoming a Strategic Leader is a brilliant intersection of proven science and astute observation. The authors' program has the potential to radically transform leadership training and development. This will be must-have reading for my team.

—**KARL C. JOHNSON JR.,** PRESIDENT AND CHIEF FINANCIAL OFFICER, DIVERSIFIED CHEMICAL TECHNOLOGIES, INC.

Becoming a Strategic Leader provides a clear invitation for leaders to do something powerful with the insights from their personality as it drives value. This book will empower leaders to make the best choices for their lives and careers as they grow as leaders.

—**BRADLEY BRUMMEL, PhD,** PROFESSOR OF PSYCHOLOGY, UNIVERSITY OF HOUSTON, HOUSTON, TX

Becoming a Strategic Leader goes beyond offering a leadership model that others should imitate. It also offers insights and tools to help leaders recognize when they are at their best, and leverage those strengths to add strategic value to their teams and organizations. This strengths-based approach is the key to developing authentic leadership skills that last!

—**TAMARA S. LYN, PhD, ABPP,** WARDEN (RETIRED), FEDERAL BUREAU OF PRISONS

This book is filled with tools, including simple yet thorough self-assessments, an understandable and usable model for strategic leadership, and practical, implementable actions readers can take to be better individuals and leaders.

—**JILL B. SMART, MBA,** (UNIVERSITY OF CHICAGO, CHICAGO, IL); BS (BUSINESS ADMINISTRATION, UNIVERSITY OF ILLINOIS AT URBANA-CHAMPAIGN); FORMER CHIEF HUMAN RESOURCES OFFICER, ACCENTURE; PRESIDENT EMERITUS, NATIONAL ACADEMY OF HUMAN RESOURCES

D1552519

BECOMING
a **STRATEGIC**
LEADER

BECOMING

a STRATEGIC

LEADER

CAPITALIZE *on the* POWER

of YOUR PERSONALITY

GEORGE W. WATTS, EdD

& **LAURIE BLAZEK**, MBA

 AMERICAN PSYCHOLOGICAL ASSOCIATION

The opinions and statements published are the responsibility of the authors, and such opinions and statements do not necessarily represent the policies of the American Psychological Association.

Published by
American Psychological Association
750 First Street, NE
Washington, DC 20002
https://www.apa.org

Order Department
https://www.apa.org/pubs/books
order@apa.org

Typeset in Charter and Interstate by Circle Graphics, Inc., Reisterstown, MD

Printer: Gasch Printing, Odenton, MD
Cover Designer: Mark Karis

Library of Congress Cataloging-in-Publication Data

Names: Watts, George W., author. | Blazek, Laurie, author.
Title: Becoming a strategic leader : capitalize on the power of your
  personality / George W. Watts and Laurie Blazek.
Description: Washington, DC : American Psychological Association, [2024] |
  Includes bibliographical references and index.
Identifiers: LCCN 2023021087 (print) | LCCN 2023021088 (ebook) | ISBN
  9781433843068 (hardcover) | ISBN 9781433843075 (ebook)
Subjects: LCSH: Leadership--Psychological aspects. | Leadership.
Classification: LCC BF637.L4 W38 2024 (print) | LCC BF637.L4 (ebook) |
  DDC 158/.4--dc23/eng/20230802
LC record available at https://lccn.loc.gov/2023021087
LC ebook record available at https://lccn.loc.gov/2023021088

https://doi.org/10.1037/0000391-000

Printed in the United States of America

10 9 8 7 6 5 4 3 2 1

This book is dedicated to our fathers.

Contents

Authors' Note

Becoming a Strategic Leader: Capitalize on the Power of Your Personality was written to help you become more of who you are when you're at your best. We don't believe in change: We believe in growth. Our goal for you is to collapse time—to help you grow as much in the next few months as you would in the next 10 years. The three key objectives of this book are as follows:

1. to enable you to gain an accurate and specific understanding of how you add strategic value through your personality strengths,

2. to describe a model illustrating how strategic leaders orchestrate human potential into dynamic transactional systems, and

3. to provide you with tools and building blocks to hone your natural talents and your leadership and coaching skills.

Visualize your greatest success. What if you could define the instinctive set of behaviors that were activated when you experienced peak performance? What if you could harness this insight and tap into the power that is distinctively yours? What if you could accurately and specifically communicate your unique brand and the ways you add strategic value? What if you could hone your skills and drive results to become a strategic leader?

In these pages, you will discover

- how the new findings in behavioral science research can help you recognize and then strategically take advantage of your greatest asset—your own personality,

- how to brand yourself so you can concentrate your career around this capability,

- how to grow and mature by managing around negative aspects of your personality that can derail your success,

- how to precisely understand how you add strategic value,

- how to orchestrate human potential into dynamic transactional systems, and

- how to strategically mentor and coach to become the inspiring leader people will remember fondly years from now.

Please note that throughout this book, first-person statements are based in the practice, professional experience, and personal observations of the first author. Additionally, the case studies are drawn from real experiences but have been altered to change the names and disguise the identities of clients to preserve their confidentiality.

BECOMING
a STRATEGIC
LEADER

INTRODUCTION

The "Aha!" Moment

I looked down at my client's psychological assessment and saw extreme personality traits. He was eccentric, hated authority, and had little regard for customs and convention. Possessing self-assured cockiness, he tended toward extroversion but was guarded emotionally; he kept a psychological distance from others. He had a very high need to control his environment, and the personality scale measuring "disliking rules" was at the 99th percentile. I thought to myself, good luck managing him!

My expertise is in executive personality assessment. Over the years, I have reviewed thousands of assessments, but these particular results were surprising. He had exceptional potential, but it was accompanied by strong career-derailing characteristics. My instincts told me that most human resources departments wouldn't bring him back for a second interview.

I had the opportunity to spend 2 hours with him, one on one. It was clear to me that behaviorally, his core personality trait matched the assessment results. He was highly creative and imaginative. His style was to pepper the discussion with direct, challenging questions, actively pursue differences of opinion, and constantly seek a new way. There was little attempt to be politically correct or to conform to conventional standards. These are all attributes

https://doi.org/10.1037/0000391-001
Becoming a Strategic Leader: Capitalize on the Power of Your Personality, by G. W. Watts & L. Blazek

of a personality trait called "open-minded." (The personality traits are discussed in Chapter 3.)

Together we reviewed his assessment, discussing areas of possible improvement and his natural leadership interaction style. Throughout the conversation I was consistently impressed with his remarkably clear sense of self-awareness. He knew his personality extremes and what they meant to him. He was able to give vivid examples of when his career success showcased his core trait of open-mindedness and when his career almost derailed because of it. He said, "My success is because I understand what I'm good at and I manage around my weaknesses. I have structured my career—no, even my life—around my personal brand."

From the assessment results alone, I considered it likely that he had been unable to find the right fit for his personality, that he either would change companies every few years or end up working for himself. His dislike of authority was a big issue, and I questioned whether he could truly be successful and thrive within a typical corporate hierarchy. Although it seemed less likely, I could also predict that he would ultimately discover a career platform that allowed his strong personality trait of open-mindedness to actually work for him.

It turns out that he did find an incredible success platform. He is currently a CEO with an annual income of almost eight figures. With so many potential obstacles working against him, I wanted to more deeply explore how his career had dramatically accelerated. What enabled him to thrive and advance to such a high level and lucrative position? According to his psychological assessment, it wasn't superior intelligence (i.e., overall IQ), nor was it emotional intelligence (EQ). Although he was quite bright and socially capable, these two characteristics didn't differentiate him from many other people who had earned the same degree, had comparable experience, or attended an even more prestigious university.

So, what was it? How was he able to tilt the odds so much in his favor? Then my "Aha!" moment occurred. There were two key factors in his success. First, he embraced and capitalized on the positive outliers in his personality assessment results, like the spike in scores indicating open-minded creativity. This is where he added real strategic value. When he was in the room, outcomes changed exponentially for the better. His unique combination of strengths— his superpower—and the active use of this superpower set him apart from everyone else. Second, he found in this position the perfect platform for his strengths and expertly drove what we call the *transaction cycle*—that is, his instinctive ability to orchestrate human potential to inspire results—which is what strategic leadership is all about.

CONTENTS OF THIS BOOK

Part I of this book will help you gain specific insight into how you uniquely add strategic value and will guide you in identifying your personality strengths and shadows. Part II introduces our strategic transacting model and presents the definition of strategic leadership. We also discuss aligning your personality traits with a career platform that capitalizes on the power of your personality. Part III continues to build on your self-knowledge and our definition of strategic leadership. Topics include increasing your emotional intelligence and listening skills, establishing resonance, and presenting to all personality types. Part IV expands on what you've learned about yourself and others to show you ways to be an effective coach and mentor. Topics include understanding your leadership style, improving your performance management, putting people in roles that maximize their personality strengths, and building an engaged culture.

ADDING STRATEGIC VALUE

Every human being has a personality. The fact that dogs, primates, and humans share similar core personality traits supports the argument that these traits are biologically and genetically based. A strong personality trait is what naturally propels us to behave in certain ways. The more extreme the trait, the more powerful it has the potential to be.

When administered valid personality tests, people's scores fall into the average range on the majority of traits. But most of us have one or two personality traits that dominate or "spike." Spiking on a particular trait can be an asset, a gift just waiting for exploitation. When people mature, the positive energy of their dominant personality traits, skills, expertise, and aptitudes emerges. Outcomes are dramatically changed because you are in the room. *This is where you add strategic value.*

Our model and philosophy on leadership development are substantially different from the positive psychology approach, which focuses on "happiness" and "virtues." You answer questions and are either put in a box or provided with a list with definitions of your positive attributes, strengths, or talents. You are supposed to gain self-insight by drawing conclusions from this information. No doubt it's interesting and fun to read positive things about your personality. Unfortunately, having this data doesn't provide you with deep insight or a road map to a successful career. It doesn't help you understand what specific activity you're engaged in when you're at your best.

We see this a lot in our coaching practice. Most professionals are highly educated and quite skilled and have had successful careers. They're good at a lot of things but are anxious and lack confidence. They often don't have a clear direction and are unsure of the next role or set of actions they should take.

When you're engaged in an activity and you're completely focused and lose track of time—when you're in the zone—you're tapping into something magical within you. We will drill down to specifically and accurately identify what makes you unique—your superpower. This is where you spike and where you add real strategic value.

PART I YOUR PERSONALITY

YOUR PERSONALITY

The first part of this book is the journey of gaining accurate self-knowledge, of pinpointing your personality strengths and the shadows that can derail you. You'll realize the power of creating a career branding statement that accurately and specifically describes who you are at your best. Finally, we examine managing and confronting the ego and discuss how to avoid falling into common ego traps.

1 LEADERSHIP DEVELOPMENT FLAWS

We've studied many leadership development programs and platforms, and we contend that there are two main failings in conventional leadership training:

1. Many programs have a fundamental basis in positive psychology, but their application in leadership development has an inherent flaw. Every strength is countered by its shadow—the immature and dark attributes of the strength. When you focus only on the positive aspects of strengths and ignore the shadows, you fail to address critical derailing issues that can sabotage a career.

2. Training for leadership development and strategic thinking is often delivered through a one-size-fits-all approach. This method encourages you to change or to imitate an ideal. Long-term results don't occur when you're asked to use a thought process or take a set of actions that aren't natural to you. It seems obvious, but asking people to be more like someone else doesn't work. It's like telling someone that they just need to get better at math!

https://doi.org/10.1037/0000391-002
Becoming a Strategic Leader: Capitalize on the Power of Your Personality, by G. W. Watts & L. Blazek

IT'S NOT JUST ABOUT STRENGTHS

Our first major departure from conventional leadership development stems from many years of experience successfully coaching senior executives who are either striving to be more effective leaders or aspiring to make it to the C-suite. These leaders are always looking to gain two insights: (a) how they can be as successful as possible and (b) what can derail them. The latter insight is one that positive psychology ignores.

Positive psychology as the basis for leadership development misses a fundamental truth. Every personality strength has a shadow, the contradictory opposite embedded within the strength. Failing to consider the shadow of your personality strength is like studying religion and focusing only on good while ignoring evil, or studying math and focusing only on positive integers and ignoring negative integers. The Chinese philosophy of yin and yang applies here. You cannot simply wish away the shadow because you want to acknowledge only the light, or the positive aspect of your personality.

In the early 1900s, the great psychoanalyst Carl Jung grasped the concept of the shadow. Jung defined the *shadow* as "the hidden, repressed, inferior, guilt-laden, morally reprehensible tendencies that lead to impoverishment in the personality." Personality measurement now has a more refined road map for how we think about human development. From this road map, we have developed a simple, science-driven methodology that will help you pinpoint the shadow to your personality strength. By knowing this, you can take a much more direct and forceful set of actions to maximize your natural gifts and reduce the influence of your shadow.

The shadow is the dark aspect of the personality strength, the paradox. When your personality strengths are evolved and mature, the shadow diminishes and becomes relatively inconsequential. It's when your personality strengths aren't mature that the shadow strongly manifests and becomes an impediment to success.

When your personality strengths are evolved and mature, the shadow diminishes and becomes relatively inconsequential.

You see the shadow every day in business settings. It's the extroverted person who is a great networker but has terrible listening skills and misses opportunities because they talk too much. It's the conscientious person who is great at managing detail and creating processes but is so focused on minutiae that their rigidity prevents them from seeing the big picture. It's the person who is great at objective reasoning but is so critical and judgmental that they lack the ability to effectively communicate. You can't simply look at strengths and ignore that the shadow exists.

You can't take advantage of your full potential unless you acknowledge and understand what can sabotage your career. You may feel good about the exercise of identifying and reading about your strengths, and why not? We all like to reflect on what's good about ourselves. The problem is that you won't grow and mature if you focus only on positive attributes and ignore potentially derailing characteristics.

Mahatma Gandhi is a perfect illustration of the power of light versus shadow as applied to leadership development. He matured in his personality strength, his agreeable nature, and his ability to resolve conflict to the point where he was able to lead millions to join a higher level, almost spiritual movement. But he was able to do this only by overcoming his shadow, which was allowing others to control him because he lacked an assertive nature. Gandhi was described as shy and withdrawn, often depressed, and unable to be critical of anybody. He even said, "I was a coward." How could a coward become one of the most fearless men in history? By overcoming his shadow! The beauty of this story—and it will be your story, too—is that he never had to change. He just needed to be more of who he was when he was at his very best.

Without exception, executives in our coaching program are interested in exploring the personality characteristics and behaviors that will hinder them from maximizing their potential. When people come to understand the concept of the shadow and the fact that it represents the immature aspect of their strongest traits, a natural phenomenon, it becomes an Aha! moment. Because the shadow phenomenon is based in science, people need not view the acknowledgment of their own shadow characteristics as stigmatizing or shameful. Viewing the shadow this way removes the discomfort and stress of identifying their so-called weaknesses. As a result, people can look at themselves more dispassionately and objectively and with less defensiveness. It's a completely different approach to professional development when you create this dynamic in a coaching discussion.

Our model of leadership development takes the whole you into account. Evolved leaders want to gain insight into their personality strengths, but they also want to know the downside of their strengths and how to negate it. Our model takes what you already know to be true about yourself and helps you take advantage of your truth. We give you practical tools in this book for shifting your thinking in order to succeed. By the time you finish reading this book, you will view your personality as a strategic weapon—a weapon that will ensure your success.

DON'T CHANGE—GROW INSTEAD

Corporate executive training and even quality MBA programs present a variety of methodologies on how to improve leadership skills. Areas taught are broad ranging and include applying strategic frameworks, acquiring innovation techniques, improving confidence in decision making, and a host of other topics. Case studies are analyzed and often highlight how amazingly a particular leader behaved under a certain set of circumstances. The takeaway is that you should emulate those traits and behaviors.

Here's the problem (the second failing in conventional leadership training): The use of generic material and case studies perpetuates the illusion that if you only changed and imitated an ideal, you'd be more successful. We contend that training must align with the innate characteristics of the individual and should not be modeled on an abstract ideal. In other words, unless the situations, concepts, strategies, or solutions resonate and connect with you on an individual and personal level, your long-term behavioral patterns will remain the same. Imitation is never as strong as the power of internal awareness.

When you're engaged in learning that relates to something you're naturally good at, you're always more open to new ways of thinking and behaving. People tend to dislike change, and this resistance is often unconscious. Temperament, habits, and specific ways of thinking are ingrained early. So, it makes sense that unconscious resistance diminishes and even disappears when learning is aligned with personality strengths and is something that feels natural to you.

When you're engaged in learning that relates to something you're naturally good at, you're always more open to new ways of thinking and behaving.

Would you rather learn more about a topic of interest, something that comes easily and naturally, or about a topic you have little or no interest in? The answer is obvious. Our point is to illustrate how your first instinct is almost always to want to learn more about or improve at something you enjoy and are already are good at. This makes sense because intuitively, you understand that you should focus your energy where it will have the greatest impact.

This point is important because tapping into your desire for personal development is where your power and potency arise. For that desire to be activated, you must personally connect to the material. This connection occurs only when you are tapping into your natural personality strengths.

Think back to when you took a course that was interesting, but you never felt a desire to continue to study or learn more deeply about that particular subject area. Compare this with a training experience on a subject you related to instantly, picked up intuitively, and wanted to learn more about. Odds are, the subject area you related to was in some way tapping into your personality strengths.

Much off-the-shelf leadership development material is not effective because it isn't customized to you. It's based on the premise that you should change and adapt to the material. Change is uncomfortable and feels unnatural; that's why people resist it. The new findings in personality research don't encourage people to change or to alter their genetics or life experiential journey. Rather, each of us has unique, genetically driven signature strengths that are reflected in our personality. With proper training, practice, and coaching, these strengths can be honed, leveraged, and used strategically to drive success.

Great leaders know that their achievements were derived not by imitation but by bringing forth their own individual best, whatever that may be. It's a huge mistake and a waste of time to bet your success on imitating someone or something that you're not. You've likely coached someone or even been coached to "just be yourself." So, we ask the obvious question: Why should leadership development be any different?

It's a huge mistake and a waste of time to bet your success on imitating someone or something that you're not.

A common objective of leadership development is to transform tactical managers into strategic leaders. Globally, this type of transformation is a big challenge for business. It's time for a new approach.

When I look around, I always learn something, and that is, to always be yourself and express yourself. To have faith in yourself. Do not go out and look for a successful personality and duplicate [them].

−Bruce Lee, *The Warrior Within: The Philosophies of Bruce Lee*

2 SELF-REFLECTION QUESTIONS AND ASSESSMENT

The following questions and the assessment that follows are designed to help you spend just a few moments in reflection.

QUESTIONS

- Is your position fulfilling, or are you looking for additional challenges?
- Do you still have room for professional development?
- Do you believe you are respected as a leader?
- Is work enjoyable, and do you feel optimistic about your future?
- Are you currently maximizing your earning potential?
- Can you identify what, if anything, is holding back your career?

https://doi.org/10.1037/0000391-003
Becoming a Strategic Leader: Capitalize on the Power of Your Personality, by G. W. Watts & L. Blazek

ASSESSMENT

1. I put time into reflecting on my personality strengths.
   a. Seldom
   b. Sometimes
   c. Usually
   d. Always

2. I place myself in situations that maximize what I'm naturally good at.
   a. Seldom
   b. Sometimes
   c. Usually
   d. Always

3. I consider myself the most mature person in the room.
   a. Seldom
   b. Sometimes
   c. Usually
   d. Always

4. I set goals and identify specific actions I need to take to achieve them.
   a. Seldom
   b. Sometimes
   c. Usually
   d. Always

5. I am consciously aware of how my leadership style is a reflection of my personality.
   a. Seldom
   b. Sometimes
   c. Usually
   d. Always

6. I consider myself to be a critical thinker.
   a. Seldom
   b. Sometimes
   c. Usually
   d. Always

7. I feel respected as a leader.
   a. Seldom
   b. Sometimes
   c. Usually
   d. Always

8. I listen more than I speak.
   a. Seldom
   b. Sometimes
   c. Usually
   d. Always

9. I spend time coaching and mentoring my people, including top performers.
   a. Seldom
   b. Sometimes
   c. Usually
   d. Always

10. I am collaborative and partner well with both internal and external constituents.
    a. Seldom
    b. Sometimes
    c. Usually
    d. Always

SELF-REFLECTION

Reflect on your answers to the questions and assessment. We suggest you make note of any potential growth areas. This book will examine these important aspects of professional development.

3

PERSONALITY TRAITS

The overall theme of Part I, Your Personality, is centered on self-awareness and self-knowledge. We're going to spend Chapters 3 through 7 examining personality strengths and then move into a discussion of shadow behaviors in Chapter 8.

We use the general terms *self-awareness* and *self-knowledge,* but there is a difference. *Self-awareness* is being mindfully composed in the moment, being in tune with what you're thinking and feeling. For example, "I'm feeling anxious right now because I know that I have to give an important presentation in 30 minutes." That's being self-aware. *Self-knowledge* is having an understanding of who you are. You might say, "I'm introverted, so I try to relax in order to be more authentic" or "I can be disagreeable, so I try to be positive and not focus just on the negative aspects of a situation." That's having self-knowledge. So even though we may use the terms in different contexts, our objective is for you to increase both your self-awareness and your self-knowledge as you read this book.

There are two key reasons why self-awareness and self-knowledge are so important.

https://doi.org/10.1037/0000391-004
Becoming a Strategic Leader: Capitalize on the Power of Your Personality, by G. W. Watts & L. Blazek

First, in our experience, people with a high degree of self-awareness and self-knowledge are better listeners. Why? Because they've gone through the process of validating themselves to themselves. Their need to interrupt is under control. When you understand and appreciate yourself and are confident in your personality strengths, you're less likely to interject or dominate conversations. You don't have to be the smartest person in the room. You're comfortable allowing others the opportunity to speak and express opinions, even when those opinions are different than yours.

In our experience, people with a high degree of self-awareness and self-knowledge are better listeners.

Second, through the power of self-awareness and self-knowledge, you'll understand how to activate positive chemistry between you and another person. It's just not enough to understand someone else's personality. You should also understand how your unique personality activates or deactivates certain aspects of another person's personality.

The meeting of two personalities is like the contact of two chemical substances: if there is any reaction, both are transformed.
                                        –Carl Jung, *Modern Man in Search of a Soul*

Ideally, you want to bring out the best in others. What if you knew the right thing to say and the right way to act to make someone feel good about themselves and their ideas? How do you feel when someone does this for you? Don't you think that tapping into this ability could potentially move your relationships to a whole new level of trust and openness? We'll discuss this later in Part III, but improved interpersonal chemistry occurs when you release your own positive energy through self-awareness. This isn't psycho-babble. It's a real phenomenon that has been validated by science.

THE BIG FIVE

After decades of research, personality theorists now agree on a general classification of personality traits. Psychology researchers have refined the list to five major independent traits, known as the "Big Five." Each Big Five trait is actually a summary of similar behaviors that describe human personality.

You can't see or touch personality; by nature, it's an abstract concept. But we can observe someone's behavior and infer that a certain personality trait caused or drove the behavior.

The Big Five classification system is used to describe behavior through personality adjectives. The model, which is valid all over the world, uses the lexicon approach, in which researchers examine a civilization's language, as encoded in a dictionary, looking for terms describing people's individual differences. Initially, researchers listed 18,000 words relating to attributes of people or their behavior. The goal was to reduce the list of terms into a standard, small, and usable number of personality adjectives that are basic tendencies of human beings.

This was a huge challenge that was initially done by hand. The pace quickened when computers allowed for factor analysis, a statistical technique that categorizes words. But this process still took many years.

There are more than 2,500 published studies referencing the Big Five personality traits. In contemporary personality research, the Big Five classification system is now the gold standard and the most accepted way to generally describe personality. The five-factor model has proven to be useful to researchers who have asked people to describe themselves in a variety of self-report studies and interpersonal settings. The model is also valid when evaluating how people describe others. It's gaining increasing use in analyses of the personality dynamics that play out in all human behavior, including on social media.

The Big Five classification system is now the gold standard and the most accepted way to generally describe personality.

Let's take a moment to ask: What is personality? In *Pattern and Growth in Personality*, personality psychologist Gordon Allport stated, "Personality is the dynamic organization within the individual of those psychophysical systems that determine [the person's] characteristic behavior and thought." Personality traits are basic tendencies that remain with us across our life span.

Over your lifetime, your behavior can and will change considerably. We all adapt our behavior to the needs and requirements of specific situations. Although it's true that everyone has the ability to modify their behavior, especially in the short run, each of us approaches life through our primary and strongest personality traits. When we have a better understanding of who we are and how we can potentially use this beautiful insight to improve our lives, we place ourselves on a more advantageous platform.

We all have some degree of awareness of our personality. We have an idea of what we're good at and what we're not good at. We know what we like and what we don't like. We feel that we get along easily with some people and not with others. The question is, How do you accelerate and deepen your self-knowledge?

THE FIVE PERSONALITY TRAITS

Let's look at each Big Five personality trait: (1) open-minded, (2) extroverted, (3) agreeable, (4) conscientious, and (5) emotionally stable. You'll see that each trait is clearly distinguishable from the next. Be aware that one trait isn't any better than another trait.

As you read the descriptions, think about yourself. How much does what you're reading about each trait apply to you?

Open-Minded

Strengths
People with the open-minded personality trait enjoy experimenting, playing with ideas, brainstorming, and debating intellectual issues. Creative and imaginative, abstract, and curious, they are deep thinkers. They are inventors and love big ideas. They are future oriented. They are adventurous risk takers and are always willing to try something new. Foreign travel, unique experiences, challenges to authority, defiance of conventions, and disregard for traditional values are usually part of the package.

Weaknesses
Open-minded people feel comfortable asking others to sacrifice for them. And their future always seems to be bright! Those who deal professionally with an open-minded person should make sure that person acknowledges the present and makes a reciprocal sacrifice for others. They often have a difficult time being and staying in the moment. They can also be scattered and lack focus. Because they are future oriented and love to speak in conceptual terms, they tend to ignore the issues and problems their vision holds for other people.

Examples of the open-minded type: Steve Jobs and Elon Musk

Extroverted

Strengths

Talkative, energetic, enthusiastic, assertive, outgoing, and sociable, people with the extroverted personality trait are energized by other people. They enjoy the excitement of crowds, seek stimulation, and get bored easily. Extroverts find the company of others invigorating and rewarding. Openly demonstrating positive feelings, they quickly make friends. They genuinely connect with others and project authenticity and trust. Often assertive, they like to speak out, take charge, and direct activities.

Weaknesses

Extroverts exist in the present and live in the moment, for the moment. They openly demonstrate feelings and alter their mood easily. Because of their socially bold nature, they're often poor listeners. Extroverts can fall prey to acting based on their emotions. They're impulsive, not reflective. They will promise performance quickly and not always deliver.

Examples of the extroverted type: Serena Williams and Bill Clinton

---

Agreeable

Strengths

People with the agreeable personality trait understand how to adapt and partner well with almost everyone. They've overcome the usual ego need for dominance and attention, allowing them to easily demonstrate emotional intelligence. Naturally concerned with cooperation and social harmony, agreeable people easily empathize and value getting along. They make strong team players. They willingly collaborate and compromise for the greater good. Pleasant to be around, they seek positive social interaction. These people harmonize and enjoy partnering with others.

Weaknesses

Tending not to suspect hidden or ulterior motives, agreeable people can be overly accepting and naive. They generally don't do well in cold, tough negotiations in which a hard-nosed approach can be an asset. Because of their nonassertive nature, they sometimes hastily and unwisely subordinate their own needs. People with the agreeable personality type are by nature nonpolitical, a characteristic that can sometimes work against them.

Examples of the agreeable type: Oprah Winfrey and Nelson Mandela

Conscientious

Strengths
People with the conscientious personality trait are thorough, dependable, hardworking, task focused, and efficient, and they are good planners. They routinely create lists and like checking off tasks as they are completed. They diligently persist at difficult or unpleasant duties. They get stuff done because they formulate processes and are determined to finish whatever they commit to. Well organized, they excel at laying out steps to make something happen. Conscientious people do their homework and are rarely unprepared.

Weaknesses
Conscientious people insist on being included, or they may work against the group or other people. They tend toward caution, acting to preserve. They can be rigid and inflexible, which sometimes makes them difficult to work with. Making a mistake and being proved wrong is their greatest fear. As a result, they can overanalyze a situation, ponder an issue far too long, and be overly cautious. They like clear time frames, predetermined processes, and measurable results.

Examples of the conscientious type: Hillary Clinton and Bill Gates

Emotionally Stable

Strengths
People with the emotionally stable personality trait are rational, objective, grounded, and not easily upset. They're steady and levelheaded under pressure. With composure, rationality, logic, and tranquility, they reassure and calm others. Challenges are coped with in a deliberative and balanced way. To underpin arguments, they like using metrics and objective measurement.

Weaknesses
Emotionally stable people are often judgmental. They can be overly tough or absolute while claiming they are making objective decisions. Their need

to assess and judge can make them challenging to work with. At times, they don't like to extend themselves for other people. They can be seen as aloof and unconcerned with the well-being of others.

Examples of the emotionally stable type: Warren Buffett and Barack Obama

---

CLUES TO YOUR TOP PERSONALITY TRAIT

Here's a way to gain insight into your top trait. What are you doing when you're having a peak experience and lose track of time? This activity may be something you do at work or in your spare time. Hobbies often reveal your natural orientation because you're doing something intuitive, something you truly enjoy.

Now think about how this activity relates to each of the Big Five personality traits. For example, if you love to visualize new ideas and use your imagination, you're likely open-minded. If you're energized by others and love to present and perform in front of people, you're probably extroverted. If you easily have sensitive exchanges with colleagues or clients, you're likely agreeable. If you love to organize and get big things done by developing processes, you're probably conscientious. If you love to assess and objectively judge data, you're likely emotionally stable.

RANK ORDER YOUR BIG FIVE

Your first challenge is rank ordering your own Big Five. Write a 1 next to the personality trait you most closely identify with. Then rank your second, third, fourth, and fifth most dominant trait. Share the Big Five definitions provided in this chapter with a few people who know you well. Ask them to rank your traits, and compare their rankings to yours.

_____ Open-minded
_____ Extroverted
_____ Agreeable
_____ Conscientious
_____ Emotionally stable

4 YOUR TOP TWO TRAITS

Key to understanding how you add strategic value is accurate insight into how your top two Big Five personality traits influence each other. In our experience, optimal performance results from the fusion of top traits. First, let's look at what business expertise capability stems from each personality trait:

- Open-minded capability is abstractness, imagination, and originality.
- Extroverted capability is initiating contact, persuading, and presenting.
- Agreeable capability is collaboration, partnering, and team building.
- Conscientious capability is delivery, detail analysis, and process development.
- Emotional stability capability is objectivity, rational assessment, and systematic decision making.

YOUR CORE STRENGTHS AND SKILLS

It's generally accepted that 10,000 hours of practice are needed to become really good at something. Imagine practicing your strengths for 10,000 hours. You'll quickly improve because you're practicing something you're naturally

https://doi.org/10.1037/0000391-005
Becoming a Strategic Leader: Capitalize on the Power of Your Personality, by G. W. Watts & L. Blazek

good at and enjoy. Now imagine practicing your weaknesses for 10,000 hours. There's no doubt you can do it, but why would you? Even after practicing to improve weaknesses, you won't make nearly as much progress because you're not tapping into your core capabilities. It's also going to be much less enjoyable and feel more like work.

We advocate playing on your home field by leveraging your own personality strengths. Your skill development will become intuitive; you will extend and develop new skills naturally.

We advocate playing on your home field by leveraging your own personality strengths.

As a child, were you pressured to take up an instrument, play a sport, or study a subject that you weren't good at and had absolutely no interest in? If so, how did it feel, and how did it work out? Do you think you could have improved with a lot of practice? Would you ever have enjoyed it enough to put the time in to really excel?

Even at a young age, elite performers love to practice skills and deepen their abilities. Tiger Woods is a good example. As a child, Tiger demonstrated a natural gift for the sport of golf. He enjoyed practicing because he was focusing on something he was naturally good at. This is when work isn't work at all. If, at the age of 4, Tiger Woods had been coached in soccer instead of golf, would he have become an elite soccer player? Perhaps, but probably not.

DESCRIPTIONS OF TOP TWO TRAIT PAIRINGS

There are 10 pairings of top two traits, and only one will apply to you. The trait you ranked Number 1 is often the most meaningful of the pair. Examine your top two traits and fuse them together. This is your personal success platform—how you add strategic value. Your Number 2–ranked trait typically follows closely behind your Number 1 trait. It will influence how the Number 1 trait manifests. In other words, your Number 2 trait activates your Number 1 trait, allowing your Number 1 trait to flourish.

You may have challenges when it comes to rank ordering your Big Five. It can be difficult choosing which trait is Number 1 versus Number 2. This is OK, because the important part lies in understanding how the fusion of your top two traits has played out in your past. Or maybe you rank highly in all five traits. If this is you, we suggest that you reflect on the definitions and examples throughout the book. Even if you rank highly in all five, you should still be able to rank order the traits.

Carefully read the summary of top two trait pairings that applies to you. Also, pay attention to the nine others, because the more you understand personality, the better you'll relate to all of them. As you read the descriptions of pairings other than your own, think of who they remind you of among your boss, colleagues, employees, clients, spouse, children, and friends. The more you deliberate and reflect on the descriptions, the greater your diagnostic power will become.

Agreeable-Conscientious or Conscientious-Agreeable

You get people to lower their defenses and communicate openly. You add strategic value by creating and implementing processes so that what is agreed on gets done. You pay close attention to detail; others know they can count on you to follow through. You're collaborative and encourage the input and contributions of others. People feel heard because you attempt to understand their point of view. You form authentic partnering relationships and are easy to work with. You're able to keep your ego in check.

Open-Minded-Agreeable or Agreeable-Open-Minded

You authentically collaborate to creatively tackle long-term issues and projects. You help clients and colleagues visualize the future and enjoy imagining through team-inspired ideas. You're collaborative and naturally bring together people with differing points of view. You add strategic value because you can mold your thinking to the perspective of others without your ego getting in the way. Because of your strong creativity and emotional intelligence, you encourage people to think about things differently.

Conscientious-Extroverted or Extroverted-Conscientious

You add strategic value by aggressively expanding the reach of your organization by approaching people and then assertively following up. You're dependable and do what you say you're going to do. You stay on top of commitments, even while having a lot of balls in the air. With a natural ability to present, you are always prepared. People energize you, and you enjoy getting out into your environment. You think out a process, are organized, and get others to buy into you and your ideas because of your enthusiasm and attention to detail.

Open-Minded-Extroverted or Extroverted-Open-Minded

You can sell the vision. Adding strategic value with your creative ideas, you have the ability to get people on board. You imagine the future and are effective at persuading people to accept your position or strategy. You have a passionate perspective and love to share it. At times you are magnetic and pull people to you. You like performing and enjoy leading strategy sessions, filling whiteboards with ideas.

Open-Minded-Conscientious or Conscientious-Open-Minded

You add strategic value by asking big questions and thinking creatively while organizing detail and processes to make an idea or concept a practical reality. Helping clients and colleagues think strategically, you follow through with a detailed plan. Your attention to detail enables you to turn big-picture ideas into workable solutions. A minimalist, you creatively analyze and distill data to identify the simplest and most effective path to follow.

Emotionally Stable-Agreeable or Agreeable-Emotionally Stable

You have an even temperament and easily develop strong relationships. You are objective and rational, yet you pay attention to interpersonal chemistry. Creating partnerships and working collaboratively are important to you. You add strategic value by getting people aligned around the best way forward while thinking nonemotionally and objectively. You look at arguments rationally, using your team-building skills and ability to empathize to get people to agree on the facts.

Emotionally Stable-Conscientious or Conscientious-Emotionally Stable

You add strategic value by staying grounded and bringing order and process to chaos. You encourage people to think about issues with rationality and objectivity, and then you create a step-by-step path to accomplish a task or goal. Process and measurement oriented and emotionally even-keeled, you work best through this fusion of traits. You pay attention to detail and like rationality endorsed by metrics. Your arguments are based on objective facts and in-depth analysis.

Extroverted-Emotionally Stable or Emotionally Stable-Extroverted

You make objective decisions based on evidence, then know how to sell or influence for your solution in the face of adversity. You add strategic value with your ability to motivate people to take action in a nonemotional way. You're naturally good at presenting and selling rational facts. Grounded in objectivity, you have emotions, yet you keep them balanced and in check.

Emotionally Stable–Open-Minded or Open-Minded–Emotionally Stable

You see the big picture and know how to focus on benchmarks to achieve a goal. You visualize scenarios; use a rational, quantitative methodology to reach each objective; and then measure the progress. You are creative, yet focused, grounded, and nonemotional. You add strategic value by imagining options and seeing multiple alternatives, then rationally assessing the optimal actions, outcomes, and solutions.

Extroverted–Agreeable or Agreeable–Extroverted

You know how to get people on the same page, rally team chemistry, and effectively energize others. People enjoy working with you because they feel valued. You are the emotional glue that holds teams, projects, and deals together. You can work a crowd, handing out business cards and handshakes. You add strategic value because you excel at bringing in new clients and partnering with them to develop long-term relationships. You deal with conflict straight on and effectively.

Fusion of Top Two Traits

Let's assume someone's Number 1 trait is agreeable and their Number 2 trait is extroverted. Their core competency is collaborating and building relationships while influencing, persuading, and selling. These top two traits describe someone who would make a good consultative salesperson who's responsible for growing existing accounts.

Now let's assume someone else's Number 1 trait is agreeable, but their Number 2 trait is conscientious. Their core competency is collaborating with others while creating or managing processes, projects, or data. These top two traits describe someone who would make a good internal auditor. By engaging people and promoting teamwork, this person will excel in managing detail and getting things done.

These are examples of two people with the same Number 1 trait, but because they have different Number 2 traits, they have different core competencies. This comparison illustrates how the Number 2 trait significantly influences how the Number 1 trait manifests.

TOP TWO TRAIT RECAP

Fusing your top two personality traits reveals your natural and preferred orientation to accomplishing work tasks. When you're using your top two traits, your energy will naturally be animated and activated because you're at your best. Don't underestimate the power of positive energy. When you're capitalizing on the power of your personality, you're sending off energy that attracts others. Don't you enjoy working with and being around positive people? Don't they sometimes make you feel good just because you're with them? It seems simple, but part of the reason for focusing on strengths is that using them makes you happy. Simply put, it's a lot of fun being great at something.

Remember, it's not just about your personality. It's also about understanding how you can most effectively interact with all different types of personalities. By the time you finish reading this book, you'll accurately know your natural personality strengths and be able to identify and speak to the core traits of others.

5 MORE ON THE BIG FIVE

Your odds of creating a successful platform in life will increase when you leverage the combined power of your Number 1– and Number 2–ranked traits. Each trait has positive attributes associated with it, and as we discuss in more depth in Chapter 8, each trait also has shadow or negative aspects.

RANK ORDER PEOPLE YOU KNOW

We'd like you to rank order the Big Five personality traits of several people you know, personally or professionally. This is initially challenging, but we encourage you to practice this exercise. You may only be able to determine someone's Number 1 and Number 5 traits. That's OK for now. Save your rankings so you can refer back to them.

The ability to rank order other people is an important skill to develop. It's important because every personality type has a preferred way of being communicated with. It's a simple fact that certain words and phrases, as well as concepts and ideas, resonate with one personality type but not another.

https://doi.org/10.1037/0000391-006
Becoming a Strategic Leader: Capitalize on the Power of Your Personality, by G. W. Watts & L. Blazek

For example, open-minded types like to visualize the future and imagine possibilities. Using language that includes big concepts and big ideas is naturally going to resonate with someone who is open-minded. Now imagine using that same type of language with someone who is conscientious. This person is naturally oriented toward detail, process, organization, and follow-through. They're not nearly as interested in whiteboarding big ideas.

> Every personality type has a preferred way of being
> communicated with.

Think back to a time when you were speaking to someone but didn't feel you were being heard. Could it be that you weren't speaking in language that resonated with that person's Number 1 trait? What about a time when someone was speaking to you, but you just weren't connecting at all with what was being said? Could it be that they weren't speaking in language that resonated with your Number 1 trait?

Establishing resonance with all types of personalities is profoundly important. Every week, you have hundreds of conversations. Obviously, they're not all critical to having a successful professional and personal life, but there's no doubt some of them are. Few people possess an awareness and understanding of how and why communication breaks down—or, conversely, why a conversation goes exceptionally well. Personality is a key factor in whether interpersonal resonance is established. Hopefully, you're beginning to understand why it's important to identify the dominant traits of others and use specific language that connects psychologically with that particular personality type.

YOUR NUMBER 5-RANKED TRAIT

Your Number 5 trait is your least-natural orientation. It's not necessarily a weakness, but it's certainly not your preferred way of being. Let's review each of the Big Five personality traits and the behavior generally associated with each when it's ranked Number 5.

Number 5 Trait: Open-Minded

Ranking open-minded as Number 5 means that yes, you can be closed-minded! You can be susceptible to being stuck on a position and not seeing the big picture. It's difficult for you to visualize more than what's in front of you. Envisioning the future is not natural; you can fall into a rut and spend too little time planning for what's around the corner. Ranking open-minded as Number 5 may indicate it's harder for you to think creatively. If you struggle with creative thinking, pay extra attention to exploring options. Encourage open dialogue among open-minded colleagues to help you to connect the dots and think outside the box.

Number 5 Trait: Extroverted

The hardest part of your job is engaging in socially bold behavior. Internal and external networking by being socially bold is challenging. A lack of extroversion can impact your ability to form relationships and coalitions within your organization. Spending too much time in your office can send a message of unapproachability. It's not easy to get out of your comfort zone and interact. You'd rather send emails than have a live conversation. When you go out into your environment, particularly to business functions, it will help to bring along an extrovert. You'll gain additional energy from their natural ability to engage others.

Number 5 Trait: Agreeable

You can bring up contrary information too quickly and create unnecessary conflict. At times, you can be overly and prematurely negative. At some point in your career, you've likely been told that you can be too critical and judgmental. Getting along with and being interested in others are a challenge. Teamwork isn't always a high priority, and your disagreeable nature can impact your ability to hold deep conversations and form collaborative relationships. If you try modifying your language to be more positive and less judgmental, you might be pleasantly surprised by the results.

Number 5 Trait: Conscientious

Creating processes and following through are not a priority. You find detail cumbersome. You avoid taking on tasks that are routine, boring, or uninteresting. You'd rather be coming up with big ideas or out interacting with clients or colleagues. You can waste time because of inefficiency, poor planning, and lack of organization. It's probably a good idea to identify go-to conscientious people you can delegate to.

Number 5 Trait: Emotionally Stable

You're easily irritated and often react emotionally. When this occurs, it unnecessarily wastes your energy and the energy of people around you. Your behavior can be a distraction and take the focus away from what really matters. Being difficult on too many occasions is a millstone. Your tendency to overreact can stifle creativity and positive energy. You have difficulty being calm and measured, and you occasionally sweat the small stuff. When this occurs, it can help to step back and consider whether the issue will matter 1 year from now. If the answer is no, then make an attempt to forget it and move on.

WHAT CAN YOU DO ABOUT YOUR NUMBER 5 TRAIT?

Your Number 5 trait can be both an asset and a liability, depending on the situation or the problem that needs to be solved. For example, ranking open-minded as Number 5 might mean you can be focused, present, and very in the moment. This can be a good thing. But low open-mindedness can also mean that at times you are challenged to accept innovative ideas and creative thinking.

Consider where your Number 5 trait might be holding you back, and ask yourself what you can do differently to help reduce any negative effects. Can you delegate work that requires your Number 5 trait to someone whose strengths match the task that needs to be done? Can you begin to migrate your role into a position that will enable you to spend more time using your top traits?

If possible, hire or surround yourself with people whose Number 1 trait is your Number 5 trait. Explore how you can either delegate to or partner with somebody who can help you offset any negative aspects of your Number 5 trait. For example, if you rank conscientious as Number 5, can you work with a highly organized administrator to be sure nothing falls through the cracks? If you rank open-minded as Number 5, can you seek out a business partner or colleague who challenges your thinking? The point is to fill in gaps and compensate for any negative attributes of your Number 5 trait so they don't hurt your career.

As you consider your Big Five rankings, you may come to discover that you're in the wrong role—for example, in a position that doesn't align specifically with your personality strengths. Many people have a high enough IQ and EQ to take on a variety of tasks and assignments. You could easily be successful in a position that doesn't require skills matching your personality strengths. But being in the wrong job is going to be less satisfying and more work for you because the work is not intuitive. The point is, if you're already in a position that aligns with your strengths, be emboldened because you're on the right track. If your position or career track isn't tapping into what you're naturally good at, use this knowledge to begin making a change.

Remember to acknowledge and manage any potential downside to your Number 5 trait, but focus the majority of your efforts on capitalizing on your personality strengths.

QUESTIONS AND REFLECTIONS REGARDING PERSONALITY TRAITS

Reflect on answers to the following questions:

- Does your current position align with your top two Big Five traits? If yes, how?
- What are you doing in your role when you love what you're doing?
- Reflect on your most successful deal or partnering relationship. In that situation, how did your top two traits contribute?
- How can you include more of your top two traits in your current job responsibilities?
- Is your Number 5–ranked trait affecting your performance? What reasonable options do you have to mitigate any negative effects?
- How does this insight into your Number 5 trait help you explain your behavior to yourself?

6 HEAD VERSUS HEART

Just as each person has five personality traits that dominate to a greater or lesser extent, each human being strikes a greater or lesser balance between rational–analytical or "head" traits and intuitive–feeling or "heart" traits. For a more head-oriented person, the emotionally stable and conscientious personality traits tend to dominate. Their principal life themes are safety and certainty. Generally, they are dispassionate, take less risk, and seek empirical evidence when making decisions. In contrast, for a more heart-oriented person, the extroverted and agreeable personality traits tend to dominate. Their principal life themes are expansion and connectivity. Acting on feelings and emotions, they don't always take data and facts into account when making decisions.

We've found that people with the open-minded personality trait can be either head or heart driven, depending on their Number 2 trait. For example, an open-minded scientist or inventor with a Number 2 trait of conscientious would be more head driven, whereas an open-minded artist or musician with a Number 2 trait of agreeable would be more heart driven.

It takes time and practice to be able to accurately rank order the Big Five personality traits of others. A useful shortcut in identifying people's

https://doi.org/10.1037/0000391-007
Becoming a Strategic Leader: Capitalize on the Power of Your Personality, by G. W. Watts & L. Blazek

personality traits is to begin by categorizing them as either head or heart driven.

Look at yourself, and consider how being either head or heart driven affects the way you make decisions. We're now going to examine the characteristics of head- and heart-driven personalities. As you read, think about how many characteristics in each category apply to you or to the people you practiced rank ordering in Chapter 5.

HEAD CHARACTERISTICS

Characteristics of a head-driven leader are as follows:

- is consistently objective and rational
- is not easily influenced
- strongly believes in their own thoughts
- has a hard time describing feelings
- tends to be emotionally independent
- does not tell others what they are doing or why
- appears calm even when intense
- does not easily give praise
- likes empiricism and is inherently skeptical
- is difficult to move off of a position

Head-driven leaders are generally more uncomfortable with feelings. They don't express what they feel, but what they think. They have strong technical expertise, possess intellectual prowess, and make decisions based on rational evidence. Head-driven leaders organize and prioritize objectives, focusing on the most worthwhile endeavors. However, their tendency to overanalyze, obsessively collecting information, instead of communicating with others can lead them to be excessively conservative and closed-minded. Head-driven leaders tend to move into roles that require quantitative methodologies or processes.

HEART CHARACTERISTICS

Characteristics of a heart-driven leader are as follows:

- is attentive to feelings and emotionally in touch with people
- enjoys open discussions, spontaneity, and different opinions
- openly demonstrates emotions and moods
- tends not to pause for reflection

- struggles to be objective and is fundamentally driven by emotions
- feels situations rather than thinks about them
- reveals much of the self through behavior
- can react too emotionally—that is, acts first, thinks later
- feels safe from self-doubt when convincing others
- has an outwardly passionate style

Heart-driven leaders are often extroverted, interpersonally effective, socially skilled, and spontaneous. Open, emotional, and emotionally reactive, they may make impulsive decisions to escape anxiety. They don't consider patience to be necessarily a virtue. They view work and the world subjectively, making visceral judgments and decisions. They roll with the punches. The heart-driven leader is stimulated and motivated by feelings and emotions; objective, quantitative facts are secondary.

APPLYING HEAD VERSUS HEART TO OTHERS

Determine whether someone is head or heart driven before you try to rank order their personality traits. Consider taking a few minutes before you meet someone new in a professional capacity to do an internet search. Review the language they have used in interviews or their online profile. Look at their job description and responsibilities, college major, and hobbies. Using this information, try to determine whether they are head or heart driven. When you meet, ask open-ended questions and look for clues that support or disprove your conclusion.

We do this before every meeting or important phone conversation. We recently reviewed a LinkedIn profile showing that a person we would be meeting was active in a number of philanthropic causes. His degree was a BA in English and communications, and his professional responsibilities included forming relationships in the area of recruiting. From this information, we anticipated that he was an agreeable extrovert and a heart-driven personality. We knew within the first few minutes of our meeting that we were correct. Having this knowledge going into the meeting was key in guiding the tone and tempo of the discussion. Because of this bit of effort and planning, we felt we knew a lot about him before we had even met.

BALANCING HEAD AND HEART

Which way do you lean? How does your own balance affect your interpersonal and leadership style?

A good head and a good heart are always a formidable combination.
—Nelson Mandela, Long Walk to Freedom

If one of your top two personality traits is head driven and the other heart driven, you're likely fairly balanced in the way you process information and make decisions. Let's say your Number 1 trait is agreeable and your Number 2 trait is conscientious. You would be someone who empathizes with others and enjoys partnering and building relationships, all while following through by managing detail and process. What a great combination of personality strengths.

Fusing head and heart characteristics into a balanced whole results in a more objective and emotionally sensitive leader. The more rational, quantitative head approach and the more intuitive, qualitative heart approach both are useful and valid.

Everyone's version of the truth is flawed because we filter it through our personality. We all have blind spots, called "defense mechanisms"; these are unconscious psychological strategies we use to make reality conform to our self-image. Maturity allows people to get out of their comfort zone and consider different points of view. Intellectual, or head-driven, people can learn to be more emotionally attuned. Feeling, or heart-driven, people can learn to be more analytical. Fusion is the middle ground—the balance of objectivity and emotions. Good ideas and decisions include both thinking and feeling: a wise head and a kind heart.

If you are overly head driven, you may not be fully aware of how your lack of emotionality is perceived. If you evaluate yourself as being too head favored,

- Try asking people, "How does this feel?" as opposed to "What do you think?"
- Work toward being less critical and quick to judge.
- Try not to "win" every interpersonal dialogue.
- Use the "yes, and . . ." technique described in Chapter 17.
- Foster emotional awareness by trying to identify what someone is feeling.
- Commit to asking one heart-driven, open-ended question in your next meeting.

If you are overly heart driven, you may not be fully aware of how your emotions can dominate your behavior. If you evaluate yourself as being too heart favored,

- Focus on being more disciplined and systematic in decision making.
- Take more time to think through detail and reflect on issues.

- Try to seek input from others before drawing conclusions.
- To eliminate personal bias, try to make decisions with less emotion.
- Seek counsel from a head-driven person who can help balance your thinking.
- Commit to asking one head-driven, open-ended question in your next meeting.

BOTH HEAD AND HEART HAVE VALUE

People are drawn to use their natural orientation; they know what style has worked for them in the past. But it's not only successes that can give you an "Aha!" experience. The "Aha!" can often result from examining your failures and identifying what led to poor decisions. The head-driven person might make a mistake because they looked only at numbers without considering cultural or human dynamics when making a decision. The heart-driven person might make a leap of faith based on their emotions and feelings, without carefully reviewing all of the data.

Appreciate the value of your opposite, and seek input from both head- and heart-driven individuals to help you balance your thinking and energy. It's not a sign of weakness to solicit the opinions and input of others: It's a sign of real maturity.

Most of the shadows of life are caused by standing in our own sunshine.
—attributed to Ralph Waldo Emerson

7 CAREER BRANDING

So far, you've learned about the Big Five personality traits, ranked your own traits, and looked at how your top two traits influence each other. Now let's get more specific about how they influence your career branding.

Creating your career brand and branding statement could be one of the most important personal growth exercises you undertake. Branding helps you look at yourself from a new and unique angle. Language is all we have to describe ourselves. Most people don't take the time to think deeply and granularly about their strengths, much less to construct a concise set of words that perfectly describes who they are at their best.

Imagine having precisely worded knowledge about yourself. A branding statement is an anchor, a daily reminder of what sets you apart from everyone else. It acts as a filter that reveals a clear sense of direction. When tasks or roles are aligned with your brand, you're tapping into your strengths. You'll be happier and more confident because you're doing what you're naturally great at.

We'll now take you through a step-by-step process to articulate your brand as precisely as language allows.

https://doi.org/10.1037/0000391-008
Becoming a Strategic Leader: Capitalize on the Power of Your Personality, by G. W. Watts & L. Blazek

What is it that you're doing when you're in the zone—when you lose track of time? What do you enjoy doing so much that you'd do it for free? What activity or activities seem effortless? What is your earliest childhood memory of success, and what specifically were you doing? Identifying what you're engaged in when you're in that zone state is the key to your brand. It's where you're at your best—where you're world class.

Parsing out the specific adjectives that describe you compels you to think deeply about yourself. We'll start with your Big Five rankings. For each of your top two traits, drill down to identify what specific adjective or descriptor best describes you. For example, if you're open-minded, are you an abstract thinker or creative? If you're extroverted, are you a performer or a connector? If you're agreeable, are you sensitive or relationship driven? If you're conscientious, are you process oriented or organized and methodical? If you're emotionally stable, are you systematic or rational and grounded?

POSITIVE DESCRIPTORS

Below are lists of 12 positive descriptors for each of the Big Five personality traits. We chose these descriptors on the basis of the Big Five literature and many years of interpreting personality assessments. We also carefully considered the nuances of each descriptor.

Choose the descriptor that best exemplifies your Number 1–ranked trait and the one that best exemplifies your Number 2–ranked trait. This pairing of descriptors will be unique to you; notice that there are 248,832 possible descriptor combinations ($12 \times 12 \times 12 \times 12 \times 12$). These two final descriptors provide you with a clarifying perspective on yourself and your natural personality strengths. The more you think about and analyze the combination of these two descriptors, the more accurate it should feel.

Review the following descriptors and pick one for your Number 1 trait. Then pick a second descriptor for your Number 2 trait.

- *Open-minded:* strategizer, abstract thinker, curious, innovator, visionary, imaginative, inspirational, original, pioneering, discoverer, creative, experimenter

- *Extroverted:* socially bold, gregarious, energizer, persuader, charismatic, engaging, connector, influencer, performer, motivator, expressive, passionate

- *Agreeable:* approachable, considerate, sensitive, empathetic, harmonizer, encourager, relationship driven, team player, compromiser, compassionate, understanding, altruistic

- *Conscientious:* doer, planner, reliable, disciplined, focused, responsible, achiever, thorough, hardworking, process oriented, organized, methodical

- *Emotionally stable:* deliberative, analytical, rational, objective, grounded, dispassionate, levelheaded, unbiased, vigilant, systematic, logical, calm

Once you've chosen your two descriptors, pair them together in the way that sounds and feels best. This is your *career brand*. After you form your career brand by pairing your two descriptors, look the descriptors up in the dictionary and write down their definitions. Think about the fusion of the two definitions and the activities you're engaged in when you're in that zone state. In crafting your career branding statement, strive to use no more than seven words. As you think through the perfect combination of words, it may be helpful to make note of other descriptors among your top two traits that also feel like you.

Once you've created a branding statement that represents who you are when you're at your best, you will begin to think accurately and consistently about your essence. This branding statement is at the core of how you add strategic value to your professional and personal ecosystem. You're no longer just a director, division head, manager, partner, engineer, accountant, or consultant. You're something much more powerful. Once you know this, you can't un-know it.

Let's look at an example. Assume your top two Big Five traits are conscientious and agreeable. Your one best descriptor under conscientious is "responsible" and your one best descriptor under agreeable is "team player." Your career brand, then, is "responsible team player." This conveys that you execute a plan or process by getting people aligned and on the same page, with abundant attention to quality and detail. Here are a few examples of career branding statements for a conscientious–agreeable person:

- I drive results through focused team effort.
- I get things done building strategic relationships.
- I build collaborative teams to deliver results.
- I deliver solutions through high-powered teams.

Your conscientious–agreeable personality makes you well suited to take on a role that facilitates collaborative teamwork to get things done. You have both discipline and focus, so you're able to reliably deliver results. Balancing your head-driven conscientiousness, you use your agreeableness to instinctively pull people together to focus on achieving a goal. You understand that teamwork and collaboration are necessary for success, and you work to create a culture of cooperation and open communication.

By creating this branding statement, you've pinpointed, as accurately as language will allow, what you're naturally good at. Knowing your strengths is a valuable intellectual insight. When you translate your specific strengths into a branding statement, you've created a powerful guide to accurate career decision making. How you add strategic value will almost always result from tapping into your natural personality strengths.

When you translate your specific strengths into a branding statement, you've created a powerful guide to accurate career decision making.

Let's look at another example. Assume your Number 1 personality trait is open-minded and your Number 2 trait is emotionally stable. For open-minded, you select "visionary," and for emotionally stable, you select "logical." Your career brand is "logical visionary." Here are a few examples of career branding statements for an open-minded–emotionally stable person:

- I interpret facts to visualize the future.
- I drive innovation through grounded rationality.
- I logically connect the dots to develop imaginative solutions.
- I use fact-based analysis to drive innovative results.

Having the logical visionary brand, you do well in situations that require using resources proficiently to examine problems that take a long time to solve. The "logical" grounds you and makes you rational and practical. The "visionary" enables you to peer into the future and imagine the situation several years out. Excellent roles exist in many different organizations for people who can use resources or design a complex process to achieve a future outcome. Visionaries like to think about and exist in the future, and logical people are rational and fact driven. The ability to bridge the two is terrific when channeled and matured.

We suggest placing your brand and your branding statement on a note-card beside your computer so that you can be inspired by it daily. This is your superpower—how you add strategic value.

I recently spoke to a vice president I had previously coached when she was interviewing for an executive vice president position at a global firm. As part of our coaching, she went through this exercise and created her unique branding statement. She even printed it out and taped it to her mirror. She shared that creating and reflecting on her branding statement was a real career breakthrough. The more she considered her own branding statement, the more she connected with it. She ultimately discovered what she was trying to understand about herself—what her true calling was.

She also shared that the previous month, her firm had put her through a 4-hour executive psychological assessment and 90-minute feedback session provided by another consulting firm. She told me that she grew more professionally and learned more about herself from our branding exercise than from the many hours of psychological testing!

In an interesting twist to this story, the executive decided to stay with her current firm. She now has a new perspective on her current position and understands how she adds strategic value. As a result of understanding her specific personality strengths, she began to reshape her job around what she loves to do and does best. She also formed internal partnerships to accomplish tasks that didn't tap into her strengths. People are noticing that she's happier and more confident. She's been told she seems more relaxed and listens more effectively. That's because she's become more comfortable with who she is.

Understanding and believing in your unique brand causes you to think and even speak about yourself differently. Consider two completely different ways to introduce yourself in a business meeting. The first is, "I am an operations vice president, and I manage shipping in our main warehouse." That description basically tells me what you do. What's missing is any portrayal of the unique aspects of who you are. Now consider another way to introduce yourself: "I am an operations vice president, and I focus my team's energy on results." If your brand happens to be "hardworking analytical," this introduction could be your career branding statement.

Which introduction is more compelling, the first or the second? Which statement would be more likely to expand the dialogue and engage the listener in asking more about you and your role? The second will, because it identifies, through the power of accurate language, who you are in specific and descriptive terms.

YOUR BRAND AND YOUR FUTURE

The career coaching in this chapter involves building your future around your career brand and career branding statement. Your brand and branding statement describe where you add strategic value. Regardless of your field, you should now define yourself by your brand—the fusion of the two descriptors—and the branding statement you've created. This exercise is designed to be an anchor that grounds you. When you're grounded, you have confidence and feel powerful. Here's the best part: The more you build your career around your brand and your branding statement, the happier you will be.

8 BEWARE OF THE SHADOW

As we travel around the world giving speeches and workshops, we often get questions about the dark side of the Big Five personality traits. Most people are interested in knowing how they can improve, and understanding one's personality strengths is an important first step. But as we stated in Chapter 1, every strength has both "light" and "shadow" attributes. To grow and mature as a leader, you can't focus only on strengths in isolation. It's inaccurate thinking to ignore the shadow aspects of your personality.

As we noted in Chapter 1, the concept of the shadow comes from the writings of Carl Jung, a Swiss psychiatrist and the founder of the school of analytical psychology. According to Jung, the shadow is best described as the dark attributes of a personality trait. The shadow, although often manifested outwardly, is contained in your unconscious. Because it's unconscious, you're not always aware of the effect of your shadow. People tend not to recognize or acknowledge their least desirable traits because they prefer to avoid looking in the mirror and seeing the negative parts of themselves. However, the more mature you are, the more open you are to discussing

https://doi.org/10.1037/0000391-009
Becoming a Strategic Leader: Capitalize on the Power of Your Personality, by G. W. Watts & L. Blazek

these aspects of your personality. Maturity means having a high level of self-knowledge.

Jung pointed out that "everyone carries a shadow." Within your strengths lie your greatest challenges. Focusing only on strengths without acknowledging the shadow is often the reason people remain stuck in their career and in life.

Your strengths carry the energy of your greatest challenges.

Make no mistake; the shadow is powerful enough to derail even a splendid career. Through an exercise later in this chapter, you'll be able to identify and see the connection between your strength and your shadow. After years of coaching and training executives, we've observed how much easier it is to accept your shadow once you understand that it simply exists in all of us. There's no need to be defensive or feel judged. You will quickly see that evolving your personality strengths is the best way to diminish the ill effects of the shadow. Don't change . . . grow!

Think of the shadow as an immature and negative aspect of a trait. In simple terms:

- The *open-minded* person's arrogance and unfocused nature make them a challenge to work with.

- The *extroverted* person's poor listening skills and ego need for constant validation make them difficult to be around.

- The *agreeable* person's inability to say no and overly accepting nature cause them to be easily manipulated.

- The *conscientious* person's rigidity and inflexibility make them difficult to engage in a collaborative dialogue.

- The *emotionally stable* person's smug negativity and critiques cause others to avoid interacting with them unless absolutely necessary.

Whether in yourself or someone else, you encounter this type of behavior every day. If the shadow and light are on a continuum, the goal is to move from the shadow toward the light.

If the shadow and light are on a continuum, the goal is to move
from the shadow toward the light.

Unchecked shadow behavior can have profound consequences:

- The shadow of the *open-minded* person is to have so many images and ideas that they lose focus and life's daily tasks don't get accomplished.

- The shadow of the *extroverted* person is to be so absorbed with the outside world that their internal personal needs go unfulfilled.

- The shadow of the *agreeable* person is to lose themselves through needing to please others.

- The shadow of the *conscientious* person is to become so deeply entrenched in habit and custom that they lose the pleasures found in individuality and spontaneity.

- The shadow of the *emotionally stable* person is to become so critical and judgmental that they feel no enjoyment in helping others.

ACKNOWLEDGING THE SHADOW

We've based our personality model of strength and shadow on the Big Five gold standard in personality research, unified with Carl Jung's concept of the shadow. Yet there are other approaches to leadership development that focus only on your "strength" or "talent" and disregard that within the strength lie your greatest challenges. We believe the shadow cannot be ignored. The shadow is why two people who have the same strength or talent can have opposite careers or paths in life. We all can think of a person we know or a public figure with enormous talent and potential who was unable to overcome the dark side of their personality.

Let's review some specific examples illustrating our point. Assume your strength is being a "connector," meaning being able to see everything as interrelated. This can be a good thing; you naturally seek to understand how events and dynamics influence one another. But the shadow of always looking for relationships can make you wishy-washy, lacking boldness and decisiveness. Leaders must eventually choose an option or make a decision. The person who hasn't matured their connectedness can spend their career in middle management because they never overcome their shadow to improve their ability to make decisions and commit to a course of action.

For another example, assume your strength is being "reliable"—that is, setting clear rules and adhering to them. This can also be good; many roles require an unwavering, reliable personality to apply uniformity. But always being consistent can lead to the shadow of rigidity, black-and-white thinking, and tunnel vision. These qualities can leave you in a purely tactical, repetitive position that you do well in but that limits your potential opportunities.

Finally, let's look at the much-celebrated strength of being "empathetic," or able to sense others' feelings. Many roles require understanding and relating to the experience of others. But the shadow of empathy is exercising poor judgment when required to make a tough call or allowing one's energy to be purely sympathetic, thus distorting the hard reality. One person's career may thrive because they were able to make grounded decisions while understanding and connecting to the feelings of others. Another person's career may stall because they continually became overly engaged in distracting minor human dynamics. The difference is that the first person confronted and negated the shadow, whereas the second person relied on immature empathy in decision making.

If you have ever taken a profile assessment and received a list of your strengths and talents, ask yourself, What is the shadow to each of my strengths, and how might they be influencing my behavior? Without engaging in introspection and understanding and managing your shadow, you cannot mature as a leader.

I am not bound to succeed, but I am bound to live up to what light I have.

—Abraham Lincoln, *The Wit and Wisdom of Abraham Lincoln*

SHADOW DESCRIPTORS

Review the following shadow descriptors, and pick one for your Number 1–ranked trait. Then, pick a second descriptor for your Number 2–ranked trait. The important part of this exercise is to see how your personality strengths carry with them a shadow.

- *Open-minded:* unfocused, distracted, defiant, impractical, dreamer, radical, eccentric, absentminded, nonconformist, scattered, unreasonable, unrealistic

- *Extroverted:* attention seeking, impulsive, poor listener, emotional, brash, aggressive, arrogant, ego driven, inconsiderate, combative, verbose, frenzied

- *Agreeable:* lenient, forgiving, easily manipulated, overly accepting, conflict avoidant, maintains the status quo, can't say no, overly familiar, poor delegator, compliant, gullible, naive

- *Conscientious:* harsh, rigid, narrow-minded, dogmatic, stubborn, micro-manager, perfectionist, obsessive, stern, inflexible, uncompromising, obstinate

- *Emotionally stable:* judgmental, controlling, critical, negative, cynical, unemotional, sarcastic, calculating, superior, smug, condescending, detached.

Let's consider an example. Assume your top two personality traits are open-minded and extroverted. For open-minded, you select "distracted," and for extroverted, you select "impulsive."

Now, place your two shadow descriptors side by side: "distracted impulsive." Take a moment to consider how your shadow has affected your career, and reflect on the connection between the descriptors. What triggers your tendency to be unable to concentrate and to act without thinking? Do you have repetitive thoughts that are distracting? Can you better practice patience and cautiousness, for example, by sending out important emails after taking a day to reflect? Or can you develop a strong routine in which you work hard for a couple of hours, then reward yourself by having a conversation and enjoying your own extroversion?

Let's take another example. Assume your top two Big Five traits are conscientious and emotionally stable. Under conscientious, you select "micro-manager," and under emotionally stable, you select "condescending."

Now, place your two shadow descriptors side by side: "condescending micromanager." Take a moment to consider how your shadow has affected your career, and reflect on the connection between the descriptors. Does your tendency to constantly check up on everything and second-guess decisions cause others to perceive you as haughty and superior? Do you use finding fault as a way to control others, or to improve your own self-image? Be open to acknowledging that others often do their job better and more creatively than you can. People will come to resent your constant supervision and critiquing. The next time you feel a need to micromanage, ask yourself whether it's really necessary. Try giving an occasional compliment, or periodically make fun of yourself, admitting that you, too, can make mistakes.

Because you've selected your Number 1 and 2 traits and your shadow descriptors yourself, the words describing your shadow behavior will be very accurate and appropriate to you. Thinking through the behaviors that manifest as a result of your shadow can help you begin to overcome their effects. Taking even small steps can make a huge difference in the long run. Just keeping the descriptors on a note card on your desk will increase your self-awareness and self-knowledge. Accurately defining the problem begins the process of solving it.

A problem well stated is a problem half-solved.

—attributed to Charles Kettering

The following are some thoughts for each personality type on overcoming related shadow behaviors:

- *Open-minded:* Direct your energy at something tangible that you can focus on. Identify a goal you want to achieve, then prioritize your activities. The act of working toward accomplishing a specific goal will help you be more disciplined. When you feel scattered and overwhelmed by all of your great ideas, assess what's really most important and realistic, what will more directly lead to a positive outcome.

- *Extroverted:* Attempt to still your brain—try to meditate every day for a minute or two at a time. Train yourself to seek less stimulation from outside your own body. Make it a goal to concentrate on what others are saying, and work to be the best listener in the room. Occasionally attempt to pause or to say nothing at all. Make note of and practice some of the listening exercises found in Chapter 17.

- *Agreeable:* Learn to accept yourself as you are, without the affirmation of others. Occasionally make decisions on your own without seeking approval. Pay attention if you're someone who always says yes before thinking through a request. Saying no might be difficult at first, but try occasionally declining invitations in order to feel as if you're more in control of your time.

- *Conscientious:* Challenge your thinking and behavior. Spend more time with people who are open-minded; they might be strategists or marketing professionals, musicians, artists, or even your imaginative children. Work a little bit every day to get out of your comfort zone. Your rigid nature may push back, but occasionally try something new. Attempt to appreciate the perspectives and thought processes of others, even though you may not always agree with them.

- *Emotionally stable:* Monitor yourself, and keep a log of incidents when you overreact or when your negativity or critical nature has an impact on the interpersonal dynamic. Check yourself every time you critique, and try giving an occasional compliment. Begin to train yourself to look for what you like about a dynamic, not what you believe needs to be improved. Try to be less quick to judge.

We suggest thinking about the shadow in a holistic way, not just as a negative energy. The truth is, understanding this dark nature helps us understand our highest nature. We can look at our other half dualistically, thinking of the shadow and light as two different and disconnected parts of our personality. But we would do better to consider the whole. Understanding our shadow teaches us the power of our light.

Understanding our shadow teaches us the power of our light.

YOUR PAST AND THE SHADOW

Just as everyone's shadow is unique, everyone's journey to overcome their shadow is unique. We often work with high-functioning, talented people who are being held back by their shadow. Lack of confidence, perfectionism, fear of not being liked or making a mistake—these are just a few of the shadows that manifest in anxiety and self-doubt. To grow means to explore where negative energy comes from and why it's there. Overcoming the shadow often involves exploring the why.

People may lack faith in themselves because their perceptions are rooted in the past. You build up memories of events—of your behavior or the behavior of others—and unconsciously allow these memories to control and define you. When you really think about it, though, the past is an illusion and exists only in your mind. If you were asked to describe past events, all you could do is provide visual images and then attempt to recount thoughts, feelings, and actions. When you allow past memories to negatively affect your present mindset, you give those memories validity. They exist only because you allow them to exist.

As coaches, we help clients put the past into context. People might cling to the past because they still remember how it felt when a particular event occurred. These scars are often carried forward from childhood and have little or no relevance to who they are today. We ascribe meaning to past events that have nothing to do with the present or the future.

Seeking to overcome shadow associated with your past means that you're 100% committed to your present and future. Experience leads to beliefs, and beliefs determine perceptions. You can change your perceptions by refusing to allow your past to dictate your present beliefs and future actions. The challenge is getting to the right mental framework to let go of the past. It might take forgiving yourself and others for any transgressions or failures. It can take time and energy to mentally reframe events and think more accurately. This process is a growth step worth taking.

OVERCOMING THE SHADOW

Once the shadow's weight and power grow in a person's psyche, their strengths and light are undermined. In the examples that follow, the shadow's potency was ultimately diminished by a focus on the power of personality strengths.

Open-Minded

Wayne originally used drugs because it was fun to experiment and "expand his mind." His open-minded nature meant that he spent much of his life unfocused and chasing ideas. Wayne possessed high intelligence and had been reasonably successful as an investment adviser. But it was all downhill once his shadow took over. Now he was in his mid-30s and on the verge of losing his job.

Wayne's "Aha!" moment came when he found his passion in socially responsible investing. It's a great idea and an emerging area that resonated deeply with him. His desire to become an expert in this investment niche stemmed from a real concern for environmental and socially conscious causes. Through his research and focus, he gradually began to see how his creativity could be directed toward something positive and meaningful. Over time, he matured and harnessed his energy. He turned things around and is now well known for being a subject matter expert. His growth came from a desire to educate others and support companies who strive to leave the world a better place. The light helped him focus his energies and negate his shadow.

Extroverted

Roger was a narcissistic bully. He was tall (6 feet 5 inches) and used his towering height to intimidate. He was smart but loud, brash, and aggressive. By contrast, the senior leaders at his international consultancy were collaborative and had created a close-knit family. At a conference, Roger was told that he was seen as a regional sales leader and not as a senior executive. Roger's biggest issue was that he didn't have the ability to connect empathetically;

he was too competitive. He believed that intimidation was power. Given the culture of the organization, his personality and management style were not viewed as executive material.

Roger's "Aha!" moment came when he turned 55. His coach at the time asked him what he wanted to be remembered for when he retired in 10 years. The answer was somewhat surprising. He stated that he wanted to be "a mentor who was respected and admired for helping other people's careers." The coach saw this willingness as an opening to grow and began working with him on how he could mature his charisma.

The coaching involved monitoring how much of the day Roger spent listening as opposed to talking. He also received couples counseling because his shadow behaviors were part of issues in his home life, too. Gradually, Roger began to connect the dots. He finally understood that he was angry that he wasn't acknowledged more, both professionally and personally. He learned to intimidate early in life, and his father, who was also very aggressive, reinforced this behavior. However, once the coach got past the bravado, he found that at his core, Roger was a good guy. He was serious about wanting to grow, and he did. He was eventually promoted to vice president before he retired. Without working on his shadow, he would have remained stuck as a regional manager. The light helped him focus his energies and negate his shadow.

Agreeable

Bob was the nice guy in the office. He was quite smart, but instead of expressing his own opinions, he agreed with everything others said. His concern for social harmony was clearly holding him back. He was uncomfortable if a team meeting got boisterously assertive. Even though he actually had a lot to say, he was almost always quiet. The culture of his organization emphasized aggressive machismo. He didn't fit in, and he knew it.

Bob's "Aha!" moment came when he experienced social injustice in his community. He witnessed someone being accosted and impulsively intervened. He loudly and forcefully demanded that the aggressor stop. Once the situation de-escalated, he began speaking to the aggressor. Bob listened well and began to understand him. In the process, he also discovered something about himself. He began to see what an asset his intellect and listening skills were. As an agreeable type, he found he had the natural ability to hold authentic conversations and ask difficult questions.

The confidence he acquired through this incident carried over into the workplace. He began to ask questions that were disarming and to get his point across in a way that he was comfortable with. More and more he was seen as a strategic thinker and as the guy asking the most important and insightful questions. As a result, people gradually began to look to him for answers. He evolved into a sincere executive whom everybody admired and wanted to work with. His power was the recognition that his agreeable nature could actually be an asset. The light helped him focus his energies and negate his shadow.

Conscientious

Brenda was an effective head of human resources. Her claim to fame was that she tied up loose ends and ran her operation like a Swiss clock. This natural propensity was based on her personality strength of being highly conscientious. She did a great job on detail and processes, but her colleagues viewed her as only a tactical administrator. No one solicited her contribution in the areas of leadership development and talent management. She was technically in the C-suite, but nobody wanted to be a real business partner with her.

Brenda's "Aha!" moment came at age 45 when she realized her career had peaked. Through coaching, Brenda began to gain self-insight. She realized that she was always the "responsible" person whom everyone counted on to get things done. Her rigid thinking was in fact an asset that put things in good working order. But gradually she began to understand that her no-margin-for-error mentality was holding her back. Her insistence on perfection resulted in a lack of collaboration, creativity, and critical thinking.

To begin the process of transforming this shadow behavior, Brenda's coach challenged her to do something she had never done before, something completely spontaneous. She decided to bicycle the back roads of Europe with no plan whatsoever. Every day became an adventure, and ultimately she realized that she could enjoy being flexible and spontaneous. This story has a happy ending. She met an open-minded artist, got married, and now runs her husband's successful art gallery. The light helped her focus her energies and negate her shadow.

Emotionally Stable

Sarah was the global head of operations for a multinational conglomerate. She was bright, but very critical and judgmental. She had a natural tendency to be negative and was viewed internally as a complainer. When her coach asked what she was seeking, she said she was tired of being perceived of as "difficult." She explained that colleagues regarded her as bright and competent, but she knew people were avoiding her. She hated how that felt. She was tired of blaming others and looking at life with a glass-half-empty mentality.

Sarah's "Aha!" moment came when a friend invited her to help serve a holiday dinner to people experiencing homelessness. All day she tended to others and listened to their stories. She saw them as struggling human beings who had lost hope. For the first time in years, she felt a tremendous sense of empathy. She wanted to help but realized that to help others, she needed to become positive herself. She had to adjust her negative attitude and work toward a change in mindset. The first step was acknowledging that each person has a valuable contribution to make.

By helping those less fortunate, Sarah learned the power of giving. Her critical nature, on which she based her feelings of superiority, began to recede. She greatly matured and became the type of executive that people went to for coaching. The light helped her focus her energies and negate her shadow.

OVERCOMING THE SHADOW

It's common to avoid confronting the negative aspects of our own personality. Focusing on what makes you world class is a much more enjoyable activity!

Everyone has shadow behaviors that need to be managed, however. We want you to feel a sense of clarity, and perhaps relief, now that you've specifically identified yours. Acknowledging your shadow is the first step toward refocusing energy away from the shadow toward the light.

If you don't have any shadows, you're not standing in the light.

−Lady Gaga, on Twitter

9 OVERCOMING THE EGO TO THINK ACCURATELY

Guided introspection helps you understand who you are—not to judge, but to enlighten. Self-knowledge shakes up your ego. Acquired self-knowledge is necessary to break down defenses the ego erects when you attempt to grow and deepen maturity. The psyche evolves through moments of great clarity. Recall a time when you entirely misperceived a set of events. Eventually, you were forced to confront yourself with the truth. Although painful, your psyche grew from that experience.

WHAT IS EGO?

The ego is an unconscious projection of what you want others to think and feel about you. Managing your ego is an important aspect of psychological maturity and becoming a strategic leader. You are responsible for what you believe and how you behave. Accurate self-knowledge helps you become your more authentic self.

https://doi.org/10.1037/0000391-010
Becoming a Strategic Leader: Capitalize on the Power of Your Personality, by G. W. Watts & L. Blazek

We often hear people claim that they are one way at work and another way at home. This incongruency is taxing to the psyche. You don't want to be different people at different times. Yes, we all have to be emotionally intelligent by altering our presentation and communication style, adjusting them to specific circumstances. But being yourself and not projecting your ego is wonderfully freeing. It allows you to be fully present. These mature human qualities have become increasingly highly valued.

Gaining accurate self-knowledge includes confronting your ego. The ego is challenging to overcome. People believe that ambition is intimately tied to ego—they would be correct. But we work with leaders every day who want to use their position of power and influence to inspire others and drive success through optimizing human talent. Their egos are very much under control. Because of that, people enjoy working for them.

In our experience, people who cultivate acquiring self-knowledge enjoy a more fulfilling career. They connect their role to something bigger than themselves. Unquestionably, leaders with inflated egos driven by dominance can ascend to senior ranks. But often, when closely examined, ego-driven dominance results in professional and personal chaos. Maturing the ego is a growth step toward a more deeply meaningful life.

CONFIDENCE VERSUS EGO: WHAT'S THE DIFFERENCE?

What is the difference between being confident and being egotistical? An insightful coaching client recently asked us this important question. It deserves a thoughtful response.

The distinction between exhibiting confidence and projecting the ego is often misunderstood. Confusion arises because behaviorally, displaying confidence and projecting the ego can appear to be similar. In reality, they couldn't be more different. Confidence and ego are actually opposite manifestations of the psyche.

Confidence and ego are actually opposite manifestations of the psyche.

Confidence reflects the feeling of the truth of something. It's a sense of self-assuredness arising from an honest appreciation of your own qualities and abilities. Confidence stems from accurately understanding how you uniquely add strategic value: You *know* who you are when you're at your best. Confident people accept their natural talents. They want to get better and to help those around them get better. When you're confident, you're not jealous. Confidence anchors you. It instills meaning and purpose in your professional and personal life.

The ego is the opposite. It operates purely out of self-interest. It seeks constant approval and validation and accepts no responsibility for improvement. The ego always comes from unconscious fear—of not being admired, of losing power, of not being liked, of making a mistake. But fear always limits what you can become. We coach people that to lose the ego is to lose nothing!

The ego has been referred to as the psyche's "trickster," a charlatan or imposter. It poses as the real you when it's really not you. The ego causes you to lie or overstate achievements and rationalize your behavior. Ego exists to feel superior and demands admiration without underlying substance.

We're all vulnerable to an inflated sense of self. When we look for praise and admiration, it's the ego. When we're envious or seeking attention, it's the ego. The ego's purpose is comparison with others. When we fall short, we can lose confidence and feel anxious. Voices in our head tell us we're not good enough. When we perceive we're better than others, this temporarily provides a sense of superiority. This feeling, however, doesn't last. That's why the ego is known as the trickster. You thought feeling superior would lead to higher self-esteem. Instead, superiority evaporates over time because the feeling isn't growth producing. Like a sandcastle at high tide, it quickly washes away.

THE BIG FIVE AND EGO TRAPS

Because personality contains five broad categories, it naturally follows that the ego reveals itself in five broad ways, too. We call them *ego traps*. Bearing in mind your Number 1–ranked and Number 2–ranked personality traits, reflect on the following:

- *Open-minded:* Your ego trap is the need to be superior. The fear is that your vision, creativity, or original thinking won't be acknowledged and you won't obtain the status you believe you're entitled to.

- *Extroverted:* Your ego trap is the need to be admired. The fear is that you won't receive the praise, recognition, and popularity you feel you so richly deserve.

- *Agreeable:* Your ego trap is the need to be liked. The fear is that you won't be included and that your desire for collaboration and partnering won't be reciprocated.

- *Conscientious:* Your ego trap is the need to be perfect. The fear is making an error, particularly in public, and not being seen as faultless.

- *Emotionally stable:* Your ego trap is the need to win. The fear is that your judgments won't prevail and you won't emerge the victor.

OVERCOMING THE EGO

Acknowledging your strengths, expressed through your career brand and branding statement, is not egotistical. Use your unique gifts to help others on their career and life journey. When you do this, you're overcoming the ego. You're also giving away something more valuable than money. Sharing your strengths is immensely empowering. The more deeply you know your strengths, the more ways you'll discover how to share them.

A coaching client told me this story about how she consciously overcame her ego:

> I was starting a new position and had a discussion with my boss. She said that the way to be successful at the firm was to put my head down, deliver quality, and reduce errors. After coaching and reflecting on the conversation, I realized my boss was unconsciously projecting her personality trait of conscientiousness. In her eyes, my extroversion was not as valuable as her conscientiousness. Her ego-driven advice was to become more like her!
>
> Knowing this and knowing how I add strategic value made a huge difference in my success. I knew that conscientious was not my strongest trait, so I shaped my job around what I do best, client contact and upselling. I delegated process and detail to someone far more orderly and careful than I am. Delegating meant that every Monday, I had an accurate and detailed report prepared for the boss. My account grew dramatically because I was upselling and doing what I do best. My boss was happy because she was getting her reports on time. The person doing the weekly reports was happy because her work was being showcased.

This is a real-life example of ego maturity. This client overcame her ego need for control and understood she could be most successful by delegating work she really didn't want to do in the first place.

Additionally, she gave away her strength of extroversion by taking an introverted but agreeable colleague to a very important client conference. She purposefully introduced him to a number of potential clients. She knew that once he had a warm introduction, he'd be in his sweet spot. His relationship development skills eventually converted one of the prospects she introduced him to into a huge client. He got credit for bringing the deal home.

He has told me that every day he thinks about me and how grateful he is for my selflessness. I can't tell you how good this makes me feel. I used my strength to alter the trajectory of a person's career. That's worth a lot!

What a great example of overcoming the ego. When you share your strength, you always grow!

The purpose of life is to discover your gift; the work of life is to develop it; and the meaning of life is to give your gift away.
—David Viscott, *Finding Your Strength in Difficult Times: A Book of Meditations*

A final, powerful way to think about overcoming the ego is through the diversity, equity, and inclusion (DEI) approach. DEI is an umbrella term that encapsulates the programs, policies, practices, and outcomes of establishing a diverse, equitable, and inclusive culture that is accepting of all ethnicities and sexual orientations. The economic advantages of this perspective are plentiful. Here we want to describe the importance of DEI beyond the current discourse by examining the underlying mindset.

DEI is a powerful approach to overcoming the ego. One of our coaching principles is that equality establishes inclusion. In other words, unless you see everyone as being equal, you will feel superior to some people and inferior to others. This perception invites the ego to take control because it's comparing you to everybody else. The advanced mindset of equality is a mature aspect of a strategic leader's psyche. It's when the leader takes time to listen to a frontline worker as carefully as when listening to a board member. Our coaching advice is to pay attention to this approach. Work to avoid feeling superior or inferior to anyone. Sure, some of humanity is more gifted and successful, but this doesn't make them better. There is no hierarchy of humanity. Don't fall victim to this inaccurate thinking, or your ego will have a field day with your psyche!

10 THE BIG FIVE–RECAP

The Big Five personality classification system is such an important tool to have in your toolbox. It's simple, easy to understand, and accurate. When use of the Big Five becomes second nature, you'll have a means of quickly understanding and predicting people's behavior, thus improving how you relate to and communicate with all types of personalities. Think about the competitive advantage this will give you.

Personality dynamics exist within every business environment. Every day we unconsciously project our own personality. How you manage people with the various personality types, especially those different from your own, affects your ability to motivate and inspire strong performance. Let's review detailed descriptions of each personality type.

OPEN-MINDED

Creating and innovating motivate open-minded people. They strive for renewal and creativity. Visualizing 2, 3, and 5 years out, their time orientation is the future. Their psychological need is for control, and they like to direct the

https://doi.org/10.1037/0000391-011
Becoming a Strategic Leader: Capitalize on the Power of Your Personality, by G. W. Watts & L. Blazek

vision. They are interpersonally assertive, speaking and acting with conviction. Their strength is their ego need for individuality. As with all strengths, when the shadow dominates, being open-minded can also be a weakness. It's possible for an open-minded person to be so much of a free spirit that they have difficulty fitting into team dynamics. Their positive temperament is being optimistic and holding a strong hope for the future. Their negative temperament is brooding, becoming arrogant, and being overconfident in their beliefs. They learn best by thinking and pondering, but they can be preoccupied, scattered, and self-absorbed. With an open-minded person, either you are an equal partner or you will be dismissed and considered irrelevant.

EXTROVERTED

Presenting to and connecting with others motivate extroverted people. Their time orientation is the present, the here and now, today. Their psychological need is for optimism and trust; being positive is important. Their interpersonal interface or style is to make promises, so watch out for the extrovert: They are quick to agree, but despite their good intentions, they don't always deliver on what they commit to. Social boldness is a natural strength, but at times they take it too far. Extroverts are often regarded as impulsive, pushy, and aggressive. They can lack good listening skills because of their gregarious nature and their ego need for attention. Their positive temperament is sociability and being outgoing, but they can easily become overly emotional. They learn best by talking and by presenting or being presented to. They appreciate, and have a dominant need for, independence and freedom.

AGREEABLE

Cooperating, working within a team, and combining forces motivate agreeable people. They are easygoing and comfortable with all time frames. Their psychological need is for alliances and relationships. Their interpersonal interface is to empathize and attempt to understand the feelings of the other person. Their positive temperament is to be congenial and friendly. Their strength is in seeking compromise, but they can, at times, be taken advantage of. A need to please and to create an atmosphere of social harmony can sometimes work against them. Their negative disposition is to withdraw and avoid people or issues. They learn best by listening. Their dominant need is for affiliation and participation in positive team dynamics.

CONSCIENTIOUS

Fulfilling or achieving a set of objectives motivates conscientious people. Their time orientation is today and in the near future. Their psychological need is for order and process. They like to create lists, and their interpersonal interface is to request or seek information. Their biggest fear is making a mistake. Their strength is an ability to create and deliver a process, and their weakness is rigidity and closed-mindedness. Their positive temperament is pure determination and rigorous self-discipline. When these qualities dominate, however, conscientious people can be seen as inflexible. They learn best by preparing and taking action. Their dominant need is for order and consistency.

EMOTIONALLY STABLE

Evaluating, measuring, and perfecting something motivate emotionally stable people. Their time orientation is the past and the history of what led to the present circumstances. Their psychological need is to be correct and to pass judgment. Their interpersonal interface is to assess. Their strength is rational thinking and deliberate decision making. Their weakness is a lack of appreciation for the importance of emotions in making decisions and formulating opinions. Their positive temperament is their balance and objective dispassion. They can also be skeptical, overly critical, and quick to judge. They learn best by reading, examining data, and reflecting on what a fact pattern reveals. Their dominant need is security.

THE BIG FIVE AND LEADERSHIP

If you closely read these five descriptions, it's clear that people with different personality traits are seeking something different from their professional environment. The Big Five is an important tool for leaders in the 21st century.

PART **II** STRATEGIC
LEADERSHIP

STRATEGIC LEADERSHIP

Part I, Your Personality, was all about self-awareness and self-knowledge, understanding and capitalizing on your core personality strengths, and diminishing the impact of your Number 5–ranked trait and shadow.

Part II, Strategic Leadership, introduces our strategic transacting model. The model places each personality trait with a key phase of the transaction cycle. Strategic leaders intuitively understand this model and instinctively use it. To successfully drive results, you want to operate on the optimal platform. In Part II, we also provide examples of clients whose dominant personality traits were successfully aligned with a business model, timing, challenges, and opportunities.

11 THE STRATEGIC TRANSACTING MODEL

So . . . what is a strategic leader? Our definition of a strategic leader began with our discovery that the Big Five personality traits powerfully align with five human-driven transactional initiatives or phases.

As you now know, everyone has each of the Big Five traits embedded in their personality. Most of us have one or two personality traits that dominate, or "spike." You'll see in our model that each person adds the most strategic value when placed in a role aligned with that spike. This role is where you're tapping into natural abilities. This is where you're at your best.

The distinction between adding strategic value and being a strategic leader relates to driving business outcomes. Only strategic leaders understand how to both optimize human talent and drive the economic transaction cycle to obtain superior results. They orchestrate human potential into dynamic transactional systems.

We refer to this revelation as the *strategic transacting model*. The model is

- a road map to optimize human talent. The model specifically pinpoints personality strengths so people are placed in roles where they capitalize on the power of their strengths and where they add the most strategic value.

https://doi.org/10.1037/0000391-012
Becoming a Strategic Leader: Capitalize on the Power of Your Personality, by G. W. Watts & L. Blazek

- a clear way to visualize the big picture. The model shows how to create healthier, higher functioning, and longer lasting dynamic business enterprises.

- an organizational development tool. The model provides a way to improve or transform existing dynamics.

Strategic leaders orchestrate human potential into dynamic transactional systems.

THE TRANSACTION CYCLE

Every successful consultative transaction consists of five phases, all of which need to transpire. The phases in the transaction cycle look like this:

1. A company creates an innovative product or service.
2. This product or service is marketed, presented, and sold to a buyer.
3. Partnering begins as trust and communication deepen and problem solving occurs.
4. The product or service is delivered.
5. The buyer and the seller assess the transaction, and changes, if any, are made.

Figure 11.1 illustrates how these five steps form the transaction cycle.

Movement around the cycle might not always be smooth. It's possible you will never get past the presentation phase, or that you will need to rework a proposal many times. You may experience unexpected issues in fulfillment such that the original scope of the project, product, or service is significantly changed. The challenge is to complete the cycle as quickly, efficiently, and profitably as possible.

What's clear is that people play different roles as they move through the transaction cycle. Unless you run a small business, the person who creates the product or service is unlikely to be the same person who presents and sells it to the client. The fulfillment phase typically requires someone, or a team of people, with technical expertise to deliver the specifics of what has been sold. In the final phase, a person, or a number of people, will make an assessment of the deliverable or end result, and they may or may not execute reinvention. Although you and your team may participate in and focus on only one phase of the transaction cycle, as a strategic leader you have an intuitive understanding of the big picture—the entire cycle.

FIGURE 11.1. Transaction Cycle

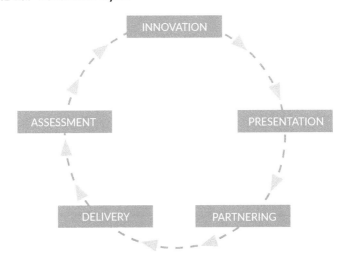

What's clear is that people play different roles as they move through the transaction cycle.

In summary, the circle in Figure 11.1 represents the transaction cycle. It encompasses the five phases or sets of activities that holistically represent transacting in business ecosystems.

THE TRANSACTIONAL STAR

Different skills are required to successfully complete each phase of the transaction cycle. Even if you are an entrepreneur or sole proprietor and are responsible for more than one phase, your individual personality strengths will be optimized in a particular phase of the cycle. Many start-ups fail because the owner–operator doesn't recognize where their individual strengths lie and where they need to bring in talent to fill in the gaps. It's necessary to cover all phases of the cycle, even those you don't enjoy or have no expertise in. We've previously advocated for delegating or hiring someone with your Number 4 or 5 trait to compensate for skills you lack, and this is why.

Each point of the five-point transactional star represents one of the Big Five personality traits, as shown in Figure 11.2. The circle encapsulates the star's five points, forming the strategic transacting model.

In the strategic transacting model, the Big Five personality traits match to the five transactional phases. In other words, dominant personality traits are most aligned with a particular phase of the transaction cycle. It's in this phase that each person can best capitalize on the power of their personality to add strategic value.

Open-Minded

The cycle starts with the open-minded trait at the top of the star. The personality strengths of open-minded people are optimized at the point on the transaction cycle we call "innovate." Companies continually invent and reinvent their products and services. "Innovate" is the word that encapsulates a set of activities using imagination, creativity, and the generation of new ideas.

Open-minded personalities are best used when new products, markets, strategies, or ideas are being developed. An experimenting and curious nature enables them to visualize things that others don't see. They're able to think outside the box, push boundaries, and challenge the status quo.

Open-minded people are most innovative while brainstorming, developing new ideas, or conceptualizing a solution to a problem or breakdown.

FIGURE 11.2. Strategic Transacting Model

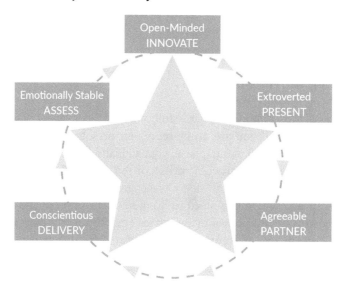

Ideas can be based on existing models and processes or can be radically new, stretching a company's capabilities. The strengths of an open-minded leader are maximized when responsibilities focus on initiatives involving innovation and creativity.

Extroverted

The second trait is extroverted. The personality strengths of extroverted people are optimized at the point on the transaction cycle we call "present." Extroversion is socially bold behavior that translates into presenting and influencing others and making lots of offers to transact.

Extroverted personalities are best used when enhancing the business development effort. People energize extroverts and enjoy being around them. Engaging with existing clients, developing leads, and closing new business are where extroverts excel. They are passionate by nature, and that passion motivates others. They tend to have strong emotional resilience, so it's natural for them to create optimism and encourage activities, resulting in the expansion of their business ecosystem.

Extroverts' charisma and enthusiasm energize and inspire people to take action. They're always looking for ways to use their social boldness to grow and expand connections. Because of their sociability, they'll naturally insert themselves in all areas of the transaction cycle to problem solve and ensure that things go smoothly. The strengths of an extroverted leader are maximized when responsibilities focus on initiatives involving business expansion, interpersonal dynamics, influencing, persuading, and presenting.

Agreeable

The third trait is agreeable. The personality strengths of agreeable people are optimized at the point on the transaction cycle we call "partner." Long-term strategic relationships are important to most businesses. *Partnering* is the evolution and development of successful synergistic relationships.

Agreeable personalities are best used when partnering and collaborating. These individuals have a natural ability to empathize and understand emotions, develop interpersonal chemistry, and promote social harmony. They exhibit strong listening skills and manage conflict well. Striving for cooperation, they are valuable as team players. People feel connected to them and their natural empathy, resulting in the ability to form deep, sustainable bonds.

Agreeable people easily establish trust and generally have high emotional intelligence. They lead by example, creating a culture that exhibits and values teamwork and collaboration. Working through conflict, they build solid relationships with internal colleagues and external constituents. They build trust through authentic communication and genuine interest in others. The strengths of an agreeable leader are maximized when their responsibilities focus on collaborating, partnering, deepening relationships, understanding the perspective of others, and managing interpersonal conflict.

Conscientious

The fourth trait is conscientious. The personality strengths of conscientious people are optimized at the point on the transaction cycle we call "deliver." All providers of goods and services must follow through on what has been sold by delivering the agreed-on products or services. Conscientious behavior translates into follow-through via the activity of quality fulfillment.

Conscientious personalities are best used when enhancing delivery. These individuals are organized, disciplined, responsible, and hardworking. They are excellent at designing processes and making sure plans are executed. Task focused, they work best when they have direct responsibility and control. Conscientious people strive to deliver quality, and they follow through on commitments.

Conscientious types exhibit strong focus and discipline, process orientation, and commitment to excellence. These attributes can drive both the top and bottom lines. Their vision, driven by a detail orientation, is invaluable in industries in which quality control is essential. They have the discipline to work hard and diligently carry on until the task at hand is complete. The strengths of a conscientious leader are maximized when responsibilities focus on initiatives involving complex detail and processes requiring a reliable and thorough outcome.

Emotionally Stable

The fifth and final trait is emotionally stable. The personality strengths of emotionally stable people are optimized at the point on the transaction cycle we call "assess." Assessment is the rational evaluation of the entire transaction cycle. In this phase, metrics, benchmarks, objective third-party insight, and recommendations help leaders make sound decisions on how to move forward.

Emotionally stable personalities are best used when assessing and making rational decisions based on facts. These individuals have a natural ability to take a balanced and thoughtful approach. They objectively evaluate the success or failure of a specific initiative. They collect and analyze data, review metrics, determine the effectiveness of effort, and make analytical judgments. They are rational, levelheaded under pressure, and emotionally steady.

Emotionally stable types have an objective, systematic, and nonemotional nature, ensuring that metrics will be measured accurately and effectively. Their judgment, assessment, and recommendations will drive strategy on major issues of importance. These issues could include the quality of deliverables, relationship or product profitability, and the viability of products, markets, or business lines. A dispassionate nature enables them to look objectively at data and draw conclusions without emotion. The strengths of an emotionally stable leader are maximized when responsibilities focus on metrics, objective rational analysis, and grounded fact-based decision making.

Think about a situation you were involved in when the transaction cycle either took forever to complete or did not complete at all. Did someone miss a key issue in the proposal or presentation? Was there a problem with technical aspects of the solution? Were there internal issues that resulted in delay or cost overruns? Could there have been breakdowns in liaising between the client and internal partners? Could you have foreseen what went wrong?

Let's summarize by listing the Big Five personality traits and their transactional expertise and corresponding phase:

1. *Open-minded:* Innovate
2. *Extroverted:* Present
3. *Agreeable:* Partner
4. *Conscientious:* Deliver
5. *Emotionally stable:* Assess

WHY THE STRATEGIC TRANSACTING MODEL IS IMPORTANT

It's important to understand the circle around the star in Figure 11.2. This graphic depiction of the strategic transacting model shows you how people with different personality strengths are naturally oriented toward different roles in the transaction cycle.

When reflecting on your top two personality traits, ask yourself whether you are in a leadership role that is taking advantage of your core personality strengths. Where are you on the model? You uniquely add strategic value based on the fusion of your top two traits. It's here where you're world class, where you're at your best. Are you operating on the right platform to consistently capitalize on and showcase your strengths?

In addition to reflecting on your place on the model, think about your team and how this model applies to them. We'll discuss this in detail in Part IV, but leadership is about bringing out the best in your people—making sure the right personality type is in the right role.

Leadership is about bringing out the best in your people—making sure the right personality type is in the right role.

Last, reflect on our definition of strategic leadership as optimizing talent within a system and driving successful business outcomes. Are your people providing maximum strategic value based on their strengths, and do you drive each component of the cycle to obtain superior results?

MODEL APPLICATIONS

The strategic transacting model has many applications, including helping executive teams understand themselves and the ways each person on the team adds strategic value to the whole. We recently worked with an executive team that was experiencing dysfunction and asked our firm to facilitate a team building retreat. As part of the day-long retreat, each executive completed the career branding exercise, and we then reviewed the strategic transacting model. Each person was now able to visualize the big picture and their individual place on the model. This exercise helped them appreciate how each one uniquely added strategic value and played a critical role in the team's completion of the transaction cycle.

The model facilitated deep conversations, including discussion of shadow behavior. As each person spoke about their own shadow, individual defense barriers fell. As a result of the exercise, everybody understood that there's a shadow to their personality strength. And rather than pretend it wasn't there, they made a commitment to become more mature and bigger than the issues that were holding the team back. The success of this exercise came from framing the selection of the shadow dispassionately, as scientifically based and nonemotional. People are much less defensive in addressing the issue when it's not stigmatizing or shameful, and we made it clear that everyone has shadow behaviors that need to be managed.

The model is also useful when it comes to employee selection. If you want a happy and productive workforce, make sure you hire correctly. Research is clear—people are happiest and intrinsically motivated when using their personality strengths.

Every job description tracks to a position or positions on the transaction cycle and to an optimal personality type. Interview questions should be developed with the goal of identifying the candidate whose natural personality strengths best align with the particular job responsibilities.

REVIEW: DEFINITION OF A STRATEGIC LEADER

Using the strategic transaction model as the underpinning of our definition, we define a *strategic leader* as a leader who orchestrates human potential into dynamic transactional systems. Let's break down our definition:

- *Orchestrates* means continuously arranges or directs the five economic transactional phases.
- *Human potential* is realized when people capitalize on their personality and perform in alignment with their highest self.
- *Dynamic* is characterized by continuous, productive, focused energy that drives each phase.
- *Transactional* is a mutually rewarding and beneficial economic event.
- *System* is a gestalt of interconnectedness, synthesis, and unity.

FOOTNOTE: VISIONARY AND TRANSFORMATIVE LEADERSHIP

Two popular leadership types are "visionary leaders" and "transformative leaders." We often see leaders described this way, so we wanted to take a closer look and compare both types to our definition of strategic leadership.

As we read the definitions of each type, we noticed that the adjectives and nouns describing leaders do reflect personality traits but aren't underpinned by personality theory—the Big Five. The detailed descriptions of each type of leader overlook the importance of personality spikes as a driver of success. Rather, the definitions look at business outcomes and ascribe a word ("visionary" or "transformative") to encapsulate the psychodynamic energy that created the result.

A *visionary leader* is defined as a person who is future and forward oriented, a long-term, big-picture thinker, innovative, grandiose, and a directional change agent. These people see what could be, not what currently exists. They embrace the unknown and pioneer new possibilities. Elon Musk and Steve Jobs immediately come to mind.

The visionary quality is most likely a projection of their most power-ful personality trait, open-minded fused with conscientious—they're driven toward hard work and long hours. These types gravitate toward entrepre-neurial pursuits because they often are disagreeable and tend to have a high need to control their environment. When you own the company, you can be disagreeable and controlling, and if people can't handle you, they leave. But often the vision is so compelling, and the personal reward so high, that people stay on board the exciting ride led by the visionary leader.

A *transformative leader* is defined as a person who focuses more on inspir-ing collaboration within an organization. Energetic and enthusiastic, they express and articulate the values that drive the company's goals. They listen and empathize with all levels of employees to understand their needs and concerns. They articulate the culture and purpose of the organization so that everyone feels they belong. This type of leader is engaging and typically spikes on extroversion. Often the secondary trait is agreeable, as they genu-inely care about people. A great platform for this combination of personality traits would be acquisitive or turnaround situations when a new culture needs to be championed. Examples are Lou Gerstner of IBM and Howard Schultz's return to Starbucks.

To our knowledge, there are no other models in the field of psychology that embrace fusing personality traits with an economic transactional cycle as a core design element. Our strategic transacting model is a system designed to characterize each phase of business and the transitions between them. The five stages together constitute a single, holistic story. The model represents everything that has happened and everything that hopefully will happen to keep the organization operating well into the future. For each phase, there is a meta or overarching personality trait. This trait, when matured, delivers a set of qualities and capacities that a high-functioning person with that natural strength possesses.

A strategic leader is one who understands how they individually add strate-gic value and what additional talents, based on personality traits, are necessary to drive the entire enterprise forward. It's highly possible that such leaders can't articulate what they intuitively know. The model provides a way for them to visualize what years of experience have taught them. In other words, there are world-class strategic leaders who do exactly what we are describing. In this book we are providing a context and a new language to understand what they're accomplishing.

12 YOUR PLATFORM

Just as each individual is naturally oriented to a specific point on the trans-actional cycle, leaders naturally lean into an identifiable leadership style based on their dominant personality traits. Once you're clear on your brand and how you add strategic value, you'll think with greater accuracy about how to land on a platform that capitalizes on the power of your personality. In this chapter, we provide examples in which various dominant personality traits were successfully aligned with a business model, timing, challenges, and opportunities.

PERSONALITY DRIVES LEADERSHIP STYLE

During a recent dinner with a head of human resources, we began discussing performance appraisal feedback. It's very interesting when this subject comes up in business conversations. Depending on personal experience, people almost always have strong opinions on the effectiveness and fairness of the process. Anyone who's received biased or unfair feedback in a performance appraisal understands how psychologically scarring they can be.

https://doi.org/10.1037/0000391-013
Becoming a Strategic Leader: Capitalize on the Power of Your Personality, by G. W. Watts & L. Blazek

This executive shared a meaningful story that applies directly to the topic of strategic leadership. She clearly recalled a performance appraisal years ago, when the CEO informed her that she "wasn't strategic enough." She remembered defending herself by saying that there were plenty of executives touting themselves as strategic, but there were few leaders within the company who were actually effective at getting things done. She felt this assessment of her was inaccurate, and it still bothered her years later.

This executive's Number 1 personality trait was agreeable, and her Number 2 trait was conscientious. What had happened was that the CEO didn't share those dominant traits and was projecting his own personality onto the dynamic.

Strategy reflects the very highest level of conceptual thinking. There are five major personality types, so it follows that there are five broad categories of strategic thinking, one matching each personality type. If I have an open and experimenting mind, my strategy might be to focus on "leading through innovation." If I'm an extrovert, my strategy might advocate "growth in key regional markets." If I have an agreeable personality type, my strategy might reflect "partnering and cultural change." If I'm a detail-focused and process-driven conscientious type, my strategy could be "flawless quality and execution." And if I have an introverted, metrically oriented, emotionally stable personality, my strategy might be "leading with data-driven research."

Each strategy can be effective when the circumstances, business need, and timing call for it. The real key to success is finding the right platform to use your personality and the way you naturally think strategically.

When we asked about her current strategy, the executive simply said, "for our people to feel they belong." This is a very articulate strategy statement and is most certainly reflective of her Number 1 trait, agreeable. Those of you who took basic psychology might recall Maslow's famous five-level hierarchy of needs. Belonging is the third level, where friendship, intimacy, trust, and acceptance needs are met.

In this case, our executive knew that the CEO was committed to moving the company from fulfilling customers' tactical business needs to becoming an integrated services and technology partner. In order to transform from supplier to business partner, the internal culture needed to be one of collaboration and trust, particularly at the senior level. To partner strategically with clients, most companies need to form high-functioning virtual teams and collaborate on multiple levels. This takes trust and cooperation between senior leaders. Once established, the culture of trust and cooperation then rolls down to their respective divisions.

Conceptually, the executive understood the importance of developing this type of high-functioning and trusting environment. She was transforming her organization's culture into one of belonging to drive the CEO's vision. The strategic thinking of this agreeable executive was perfectly aligned with what the company was looking to achieve.

The executive's CEO was a strong extrovert who naturally believed that "strategy" was about some kind of expansion, possibly new markets or lines of business, whereas the agreeable executive thought strategically in terms of forming deeper human connections. The CEO didn't understand this. He lacked the psychological maturity to see how his perception of strategic thinking was a projection of his personality structure.

DON'T CHANGE–GROW INSTEAD

In our executive coaching, we're often asked to help a person become more strategic. When we ask how they define "strategic," the responses are all over the map. "They need to be able to connect the dots. They need to be able to make it happen." Whatever that means! No one seems to be able to tell another person exactly how to be strategic, only that they should be.

The process of rank ordering your Big Five personality traits and selecting your positive and shadow descriptors was designed to help you understand who you are at your core and how you add strategic value. As we stated at the beginning of the book, our message is this: Change isn't what we believe leadership development is all about. We want you to be more of who you are when you're using your strengths and operating at peak performance.

We want you to be more of who you are when you're using your strengths and operating at peak performance.

Think of great artists and writers. They all have weighty subject matter expertise, but each individual is unique and exhibits their proficiency differently. These artistic differences occur because each artist or writer has a different personality and brings forth their creativity through that personality. Why should leadership coaching and training to think more creatively and strategically be any different? It shouldn't.

We touched on this earlier, but it's worth reiterating the point. Best practices reveal that skills training needs to be developed around the innate characteristics of the individual, and not modeled on an "ideal." If it's true that people perform best when tapping into their strengths, a vanilla, cookie-cutter program that doesn't individualize the curriculum to each personality type will ring hollow. Unless the concepts being taught align with and to your individual core strengths, you will experience no permanent shift in behavior. The material won't resonate if you can't visualize and integrate how it applies to you.

Creativity springs from the unconscious: That's why you can't be strategic by mimicking someone else's behavior or actions. You create the highest abstract and intuitive connections through your dominant personality trait. Asking you to change is discounting your greatest asset.

Asking you to change is discounting your greatest asset.

FINDING THE RIGHT PLATFORM

Thinking strategically is the top quality boards of directors look for in CEO candidates. Yet, boards rarely define what kind of strategy is desired. The reason many new CEOs "fail" is not because they aren't highly competent. It's because their natural strengths don't match the strengths most required in the position. Consequently, they aren't able to effectively do what strategic leaders do, which is orchestrate human potential into dynamic transactional systems.

Even when hiring senior-level executives, companies may neglect to identify the critical personality-based skills that are required. The person being considered often doesn't fully understand the business culture or challenges and the specific problems that need to be solved. In these circumstances, a costly hiring mismatch often results.

Let's assume that I have an open-minded personality and expertise in marketing strategy, and I'm brought in as a high-level executive to manage organizational development issues. I'm likely to fail, and here's why. My natural strengths are marketing a product or service in a unique and memorable way; this is reflective of my open-minded personality. My strengths aren't in holding profound discussions to identify the issues causing organizational conflict, or in aligning different divisions around a strategic vision. The agreeable personality would be much better suited for the challenges this role demands: collaboration, virtual teaming, and conflict management. After many months of struggle, it will become painfully obvious to everyone (including myself) that I'm not the right fit for the job.

The hiring fail occurs because the skills required to be successful in this situation don't match my competencies or personality strengths. Ultimately (and predictably), I'm asked to leave the organization, and the merry-go-round continues. This costly scenario plays out over and over in business.

EXAMPLES OF EXTRAORDINARY LEADERS

Let's look at two examples in which people with different dominant personality traits had extraordinary success by finding the right platform to capitalize on their strengths.

Sam Walton is revered for reinventing retail strategy. His subject matter expertise was merchandising and partner management, but it was Walton's dominant personality traits that created and drove the Walmart phenomenon.

His Number 1–ranked trait was emotionally stable, and his Number 2–ranked trait was agreeable. If we were to pick two positive descriptors from our career branding exercise for Sam Walton, they would be "logical" for emotionally stable and "relationship driven" for agreeable. His brand would be "logical relationship driven." A branding statement could be "I use common sense to bond with people."

The distinctive behavior from Walton's principal trait of emotional stability was his logical nature. He understood the rationality of offering many products under one roof and of creating a visually stimulating shopping event that people would go out of their way to experience. The company's growth strategy of expansion in rural markets wasn't visionary. It was based on replicating a logical formula. Walton's Number 2 trait of agreeable was evidenced in the way he built relationships with customers. He believed in the values of respect and fairness—he promised that their lives would be enhanced by virtue of being a customer.

Walton's strategy was replicating a formula and authentically selling the trustworthiness of Walmart as an asset to any community. It wasn't his subject matter expertise that created this strategy. It was the activation and evolved maturity of his dominant traits of emotionally stable and agreeable that led Walmart to remarkable success.

Our partnership with our associates is the reason our company has been able to consistently outperform the competition—and even our own expectations.
—Sam Walton, *Walmart World Newsletter*

Sergey Brin, cofounder of Google, has a mythological story. Brin's educated parents left Russia because being Jewish inhibited their academic freedom. He witnessed prejudice against his parents at an early age, irrevocably shaping his thinking. His core expertise is mathematics and business. He's considered a philosophical visionary.

His Number 1 trait is open-minded, and his Number 2 trait is agreeable. If we were to pick two positive descriptors from our career branding exercise for Sergey Brin, they would be "pioneering" for open-minded and "empathetic" for agreeable. His brand would be "pioneering empathetic." A branding statement could be "I revolutionize how you feel about knowledge."

Equality is the distinctive strategy derived from Brin's principal trait of open-minded. Google's mission is to even out the playing field by providing universal access to the Internet. Making free information available worldwide was a groundbreaking concept that reflects Brin's open-minded, pioneering orientation. Brin's Number 2 trait of agreeable is evidenced by his commitment to a sense of fairness. He empathized with individuals who had limited access to data. And his desire to be trusted and ethical also is an attribute of the agreeable personality trait.

Brin's strategy of making information available to everyone wasn't a reflection of his subject matter expertise in math. Rather, it was the activation and evolved maturity of his dominant traits of open-minded and agreeable that led Google to extraordinary success. If Brin had a different personality, there might never have been a Google, or Google would certainly look quite different than it does today.

Obviously everyone wants to be successful, but I want to be looked back on as being very innovative, very trusted and ethical and ultimately making a big difference in the world.

–Sergey Brin, on ABC News

Sam Walton and Sergey Brin are two very different examples of successful leaders. What do they have in common? Their strategic visions aligned with their dominant traits and core strengths, and both leaders created the perfect platform to capitalize on those strengths.

COACHING FOR A MISMATCHED PLATFORM

Recently we had an executive from a major consulting firm go through our executive coaching program. His boss was looking for him to improve his "presence." The boss was a forceful extrovert who was well known for his strong charisma and business development prowess. He wanted his direct report to become more like him (but didn't have enough self-insight to realize this).

After interviewing the client, it was obvious that his Number 1 trait was emotionally stable and his Number 2 trait was conscientious. Extroverted was his Number 5–ranked trait. Together we quickly determined that he was head driven and his boss was heart driven. It was no wonder they had difficulty getting on the same page.

The vast majority of coaches would have encouraged the executive to become more extroverted—that is, to change his basic orientation. But changing your basic orientation is a fool's errand, and this is the reason why coaching so often fails to work. The client was a good man . . . honest, sincere, and genuine. He wasn't charismatic like his boss, and he was never going to be.

Our approach was for him to embrace his emotional stability. This meant he needed to appreciate his ability to make good decisions using logic and facts. This is what confidence is—recognizing and accepting your unique strengths. The turnaround came when he did just that. Coaching gave him the confidence to move on from the organization to an executive position that was better aligned with his strengths. It's no surprise that he's happier.

> This is what confidence is—recognizing and accepting your unique strengths.

THE RIGHT PLATFORM MATTERS

You'll find confidence and power in being comfortable with your own individual strengths and leadership style. Don't let anyone suggest that you should become someone you're not.

Your dominant personality traits will drive how you add strategic value and how you naturally think strategically. Strategic leadership results from executing the strategic transacting model to orchestrate human potential into dynamic transactional systems. It will be very difficult, if not impossible, for you to accomplish strategic leadership without operating on a platform that aligns with your strengths.

PART **III** BUILDING BLOCKS OF STRATEGIC LEADERSHIP

BUILDING BLOCKS OF STRATEGIC LEADERSHIP

Now we'll continue to build upon your self-knowledge and our definition of strategic leadership. Essential to becoming a strategic leader are strong interpersonal skills and the ability to assess situations with clarity and maturity in order to guide and influence outcomes. These skills are necessary to execute the strategic transacting model—to orchestrate human potential into dynamic transactional systems. Here we'll cover establishing emotional resonance, emotional intelligence, interdependent resonance, listening, listening and body language exercises, how to influence behavior, presentation pointers, and call to action emails.

13 ESTABLISHING EMOTIONAL RESONANCE

You interact daily with a wide variety of internal and external constituents. Being able to communicate effectively with all types of personalities is key to influencing others to buy into you and your ideas. The Big Five classification is a valuable tool to help you establish resonance and motivate people to take action on your behalf.

The reason to understand someone's dominant trait is so you can speak the language of their personality strengths. The more you use language that resonates, the more they believe (and rightly so) that you relate to their perspective and frame of reference. You're using language that they're comfortable transacting in. The following topics particularly resonate with each of the Big Five personality traits:

- *Open-minded* people like to talk about the future. They think conceptually and creatively. They enjoy big ideas and thinking outside the box.

- *Extroverted* people like to talk about most anything. They enjoy making connections, presenting, and selling.

https://doi.org/10.1037/0000391-014
Becoming a Strategic Leader: Capitalize on the Power of Your Personality, by G. W. Watts & L. Blazek

- *Agreeable* people like to talk about relationships and partnering. They enjoy teamwork and cultural harmony.

- *Conscientious* people like to talk about detail, scheduling, lists, processes, and project management.

- *Emotionally stable* people like to talk about rational measurement and objective goals.

The reason to understand someone's dominant trait is so you can speak the language of their personality strengths.

In Malcolm Gladwell's best-selling book *Blink,* he writes about the adaptive unconscious—the mental processes that work rapidly and automatically with relatively little information. He discusses "thin slicing," in which your unconscious finds patterns in situations and behaviors based on very narrow slices of information. This automated unconscious process takes place in every interpersonal interaction. To ignore the occurrence of this phenomenon is to discount a key element of why people either connect or don't connect.

Let's assume I'm having a first meeting with a prospective client named John, someone whom I've established is head driven. Based on my research, I determine that his Number 1 trait is emotionally stable. John is going to be metrically inclined, so I don't want to begin our conversation by speaking conceptually about big ideas, partnering, or teamwork. Although those issues may be important to me, and they can be discussed later, they're not going to be as important to John as rationality and objective measurement. John will also engage in thin slicing, making an unconscious and rapid assessment of me, based in part on the language I use. If I speak from my frame of reference and not his, I'll lower the probability of resonating with John.

Scenarios in which resonance is never established play out in business every day. Most people have no idea what went wrong, why a meeting or presentation fell flat. When you perceive the language needs of others, molding your discussion around what's important to them, you'll be better able to connect psychologically. When you fully concentrate on someone else, your own ego stays deactivated—this is how great listening and resonance begin.

Here are additional examples for each trait:

- If you talk to an open-minded person about process and detail, you will lose them quickly. They want to think conceptually and abstractly.

- If you talk to an extroverted person about metrics or details too early, you will lose their interest. They want to socialize and experience the adrenaline rush of a new interpersonal encounter.

- If you talk to an agreeable person exclusively about business issues and not about building or expanding a relationship, they are likely to become distant. They want to experience a personal connection.

- If you focus on an elaborate, risk-taking vision with a conscientious person, they might become uncomfortable or fatigued. They are inherently cautious and want to experience certainty.

- If you talk about warm feelings with an emotionally stable person, you lose credibility. They want to experience rationality without emotions that could sway their judgment.

In summary, you'll connect on an unconscious level and establish emotional resonance more quickly if you tailor your language to the dominant personality traits of the person you are speaking to.

RESONANCE: WHAT'S REALLY HAPPENING

Other than conversation, what happens in the first several minutes, or even seconds, of meeting somebody? What gets interpersonal encounters off to a great start? Conversely, what happens when there seems to be no connection whatsoever with a person?

Resonance is a concept stemming from the new science of interpersonal neurobiology. Resonance is a neurological, chemical, and electrical compound reaction that occurs in the brain. The brain has what's referred to as an "open-loop system": Brain waves sync and people link up, becoming attuned to each other's inner states. We're wired to unconsciously pick up subtle cues and influence each other.

We're wired to unconsciously pick up subtle cues and influence each other.

Think back to a time when you've been in a room and a joyfully or negatively expressive individual enters. What happens? Does the mood or energy of the room change because others feel that individual's state of being? The answer is yes. If we allow ourselves, we can become attuned to another person's inner harmony or disharmony. Becoming attuned is easier for some personality types than others. However, leaders with strong emotional intelligence are able to understand what's happening beneath the surface, how it alters their emotional state and changes the unconscious dynamics in a room.

Neuroscience studies demonstrate that in positive and effective group dynamics, individuals' brains become fused into a collective emotional state once they begin resonating. Essentially, minds become synchronized. Trusting relationships, cooperation, and mutual empathy result. In business settings, synchronization occurs best when the leader is maturely confident. The phenomenon of people unifying into a social system activates when leaders emotionally resonate with their teams. When people are resonating, their egos are not interfering—they will be more open to new ideas and have a less guarded social orientation.

From a neuroscience perspective, teamwork is the reciprocity of positive emotions between team members, interconnecting their collective brains. Simply put, if the leader doesn't resonate with the team, then the team is merely a group of people. Exceptional performance begins to happen when people sync up neurologically. They collaborate and act with interdependency.

Simply put, if the leader doesn't resonate with the team, then the team is merely a group of people.

Scientific evidence clearly shows that in interpersonal encounters, there is much happening beneath the surface, unconsciously and on a subliminal level. Be aware that this phenomenon influences both individual and group dynamics.

14 EMOTIONAL INTELLIGENCE

You're probably familiar with the term "emotional intelligence." Even if you believe you have a solid understanding of this concept, please read on. We take a different approach to emotional intelligence by relating its components to how your behaviors manifest based on your Big Five ranking.

Emotional intelligence, or EI, is the ability to read, regulate, control, and use your emotions to positively energize interpersonal encounters. The concept of being able to get along well with others and make good interpersonal decisions is not new—it's been around since the time of Aristotle. The innate potential for high EI is contained within each personality trait. The critical attribute of EI is having the emotional maturity to *not project your dominant personality trait into the interpersonal dynamic*—that is, to not allow your shadow to manifest interpersonally. Additionally, people with high EI have the ego strength to consistently listen well. You enjoy listening because you've already validated yourself to yourself!

We advocate that high EI includes the genuine desire to ask open-ended questions and listen well. This desire enables conversations to deepen and become positively authentic. In essence, your purpose is to use your gift

https://doi.org/10.1037/0000391-015
Becoming a Strategic Leader: Capitalize on the Power of Your Personality, by G. W. Watts & L. Blazek

to help the other person grow, provide relevant insights, and elevate the discussion.

Each personality structure tends to display emotional intelligence differently. Let's examine each personality trait and analyze how EI is expressed behaviorally.

- *Open-minded:* When open-minded people have high EI, they ask questions about how the other person's future can look, about what their plans and dreams could be. They get people to creatively reflect on possibilities.

- *Extroverted:* When extroverted people have high EI, they ask questions about how the other person can win or help them think big or expand the possible outcome.

- *Agreeable:* When agreeable people have high EI, they ask questions that encourage the other person to reflect on how they feel and to get in deeper touch with their own emotions.

- *Conscientious:* When conscientious people have high EI, they ask questions about how the other person's ideas and hopes can materialize by having a process and plan in place.

- *Emotionally stable:* When emotionally stable people have high EI, they ask questions about how the other person will know they have achieved a successful outcome, about what metrics and measurement they will use.

Behavioral scientists are hard at work trying to understand how people can strengthen their emotional intelligence. As part of this research, scientists are looking to discover what part of EI is genetic and what trait or traits are drivers of high EI. We've already learned that people with different personality traits give and receive energy differently. Just because you connect with one individual doesn't mean you'll connect with another. But people with high EI are better able to adapt to other people's personalities and emotions: That's why they're emotionally intelligent!

People with high emotional intelligence are better able to adapt to other people's personalities and emotions.

Recently, I met with the executive vice president of human resources for a large Fortune 500 company. We hit it off immediately. Within minutes, you would have thought we had known each other for years. In contrast, I can recall a meeting several years ago (before we had developed our personality model) with a global head of human resources—try as I might, the conversation was labored. I felt that my behavior was much the same in both meetings, yet one encounter was so much more engaging than the other. Why? Because the two people I met with had completely different personalities.

The executive vice president's personality was similar to mine. Interpersonal resonance came easily and naturally. The global head of human resources was my complete opposite, which is why we weren't connecting. At the time, if I had understood our model, I would have altered my language and style to adapt to this person's personality. There's no doubt that making this adjustment would have improved the connection between us. When you consciously adapt your language to resonate more deeply with others, you are subordinating your ego in order to make the discussion more meaningful. This is a sign of high EI: a willingness to adapt in order to positively energize an interpersonal encounter.

On occasion, you may have difficulty establishing resonance, even when you correctly identify the person's dominant personality trait and use language that connects psychologically. There can be other factors at work, and clearly both people have to participate in the process of engagement. Having said this, we maintain that the likelihood of a successful encounter will be much greater now that you understand the five ways personality interacts and transacts. When you really know this model, you'll have a higher probability of connecting with almost everyone. And when you don't connect, you'll have a much better understanding of why. These insights are the essence of emotional intelligence.

We acknowledge that there will be people in your life who you can't please, can't make like you, and can't get on your team. That's OK. For every one person who doesn't relate to you, work to develop 10 who do.

The concept of emotional intelligence began to emerge as researchers wanted to understand what caused success outside of intellect. IQ, or intelligence quotient, is relatively fixed. EI, on the other hand, is amenable to change and can evolve. In fact, you can work to increase your EI and make fairly rapid progress.

You already know this. The "smartest person in the room" is not necessarily the person who makes the most money or has the most power. There are clearly other factors at work. We now know that once a threshold of intellect is reached, emotional intelligence becomes equally important, or perhaps even more important, than cognitive ability. It's especially valuable in new economy leadership roles where consultative relationships, interdependency, and teamwork are vital to success.

The "smartest person in the room" is not necessarily the person who makes the most money or has the most power.

CHARACTERISTICS OF EMOTIONAL INTELLIGENCE

The characteristics of emotional intelligence can be summarized as skill in managing conflict, a positive outlook, a mindset of gratitude, self-management of emotions, ego control, a habit of self-reflection, a willingness to recharge, sharpened focus, and the ability to handle stress. We'll look at each characteristic in detail and the ways dominant traits play a role in how they manifest.

Skill in Managing Conflict

Leaders with high emotional intelligence do a good job of managing interpersonal conflict. They don't back down, nor will they avoid a conversation when confronted with emotional dynamics. They identify negative feelings and work through conflict without becoming visibly distressed. Keeping their ego in check, they don't get wrapped up in the emotionality of the moment.

No doubt you've had to manage daily workplace dramas such as communication breakdowns, misunderstandings, disappointments, and occasional anger. Reflect on how you typically handle these situations and how you approach difficult interpersonal dynamics. Do you see any relationship between your actions under stress and your dominant personality traits and their shadows?

Granted, those people who rank agreeable as Number 1 will have an edge because they are naturally skilled at managing conflict, empathizing, and lowering the temperature in a room. Leaders with high emotional stability are naturally better at being dispassionate and objective. They can more easily avoid getting sucked into emotional situations. Notice how your dominant traits and their shadows manifest, and work toward becoming the most mature you can be.

Positive Outlook

People with high emotional intelligence aren't overly critical of themselves or their environment. They are mostly positive and optimistic and understand that everyone makes mistakes. The power of a positive mental attitude is validated by neuroscience. Positive, upbeat people are happier and manage stress more effectively. Wouldn't you rather be associated with or work for someone who is happy and optimistic?

Reflect on any issues in your life that activate self-condemnation. Are there negative factors in your environment, personal or professional, that influence how you feel about your ability to succeed? Is there anything you can do about them? This last question is extremely important in the context of maintaining resilience and optimism. Are there people in your personal or professional life who support and encourage you? Being around people with negative energy is a silent, debilitating force. It's more difficult to leverage strengths, have a positive outlook, and display high emotional resilience when you aren't operating in an upbeat environment or don't have a positive support system.

While I was recently coaching an executive, the conversation turned toward challenges he had been having for some time at home. Highly creative and innovative, his Number 1 trait was open-minded. When I asked whether his creativity had diminished because of his personal situation, there was a long pause. He replied that it had, but up until that moment, he hadn't really connected the two. Ultimately, the lack of a positive environment at home was absorbing his energy and negatively impacting his ability to think creatively. It wasn't surprising that this situation caused him to be unhappy; you are always happiest when you're activating your natural strengths. You can't solve a problem until you acknowledge it, so understanding the connection here was an important first step.

Mindset of Gratitude

New research has shown something amazing. When you feel gratitude and focus on the ways in which you are fortunate, you become mentally stronger. People with high EI appreciate themselves and others. They don't need constant praise or accolades to bolster their self-esteem. This grateful attitude also helps motivate and inspire those around them.

If you think this notion of gratitude is trivial, try Googling "gratitude and success." You'll find pages and pages of quotes from amazingly successful people, from John F. Kennedy, to Albert Einstein, to the Buddha. When you appreciate yourself and the opportunities around you, your fear diminishes, and you attract positive energy. How can this be a bad thing?

Self-Management of Emotions

You already know that being in a leadership role means occasional high highs and low lows. It's exciting to close a deal or to get a big project successfully over the goal line—but life being what it is, you win some and you lose some. People with high EI are steady under pressure and adversity. This doesn't mean they don't get upset or angry, but they do maintain a sense of humor and more quickly admit mistakes.

Leaders who rank emotional stability as their Number 1 trait are naturally going to be more balanced. If you ranked yourself low in emotional stability, you already understand that your emotions can sometimes get the best of you. The challenge is to catch yourself when you begin to unravel, try to adjust your behavior, and put the stressful situation into perspective.

Managing emotion and working toward becoming more even-keeled often aren't easy. A highly emotional person likely will never be as calm as a fighter pilot or heart surgeon, but that's not the goal. People with high EI proactively acknowledge their challenges and adjust their behavior accordingly.

Ego Control

We discussed the ego in detail in Chapter 9. Having your ego under control is critical to having high emotional intelligence. The ego is the part of the mind that seeks validation and recognition. It's your sense of self-importance and personal identity. It can be your best friend and your worst enemy. Your ego can fuel confidence, boldness, passion, and goal-directed behavior. Your ego can also drive unproductive, inappropriate actions that negatively impact your effectiveness.

Typically, it's our need for recognition, acknowledgment, or power, or all of the above, that throws us off when it comes to interpersonal dynamics. Think about a meeting or encounter that didn't go well. Did you, or possibly someone else, squander an opportunity by not listening, dominating the conversation, or interrupting the discussion? This is a sign of low emotional intelligence. Looking back, you may find that this behavior was a display of dominance resulting from an ego need for recognition.

Not long ago, I was in a meeting where one of our young associates was sharing a story with a client. The client interrupted and started telling her own story. I was impressed when our associate immediately pivoted and asked her an open-ended question. When interrupted, most people have a sense of incompleteness. They feel the need to complete their story, even after the person who interrupted finishes speaking. Our associate displayed no such need, allowing the client to dominate the conversation.

This associate provides an excellent example of someone who exhibited high emotional intelligence. His reaction to this situation demonstrated that he had overcome the ego need to validate himself. Consequently, it was much easier for him to be interrupted and not demand his share of "airtime."

We'll spend more time discussing listening skills in Chapters 16 and 17, but begin now to pay attention to how often people around you interrupt or dominate a conversation. If you further study their behavior, you're likely to notice other signs of low emotional intelligence. The bad habit of interrupting or needing to be the center of attention not only is annoying, but can also be a real career derailer. Once someone becomes confident in who they are, they'll have less of a need to prove how great they are to everyone else. Understanding your strengths and acknowledging your shadow behavior can actually diminish your need to feed the ego.

Habit of Self-Reflection

People with high emotional intelligence take time regularly (once a month, or at least once a quarter) to reflect on their core purpose and vision. Occasionally you'll need to go off by yourself and do some good old-fashioned introspection. Hopefully, your level of self-reflection will be deeper and more meaningful as a result of having gone through the exercise of creating your career brand and branding statement. With the world moving at such a fast pace, it's mentally healthy to take time out to reflect.

Priority on Recharging

Being empathetic, listening, keeping emotions in check, and motivating people take a lot of emotional energy. Leadership is an intensive energy-giving experience. It's important to acknowledge this and to balance work-related and personal activities. Even extroverts need time alone to recharge. Do any of these statements apply to you?

- You often check email and phone messages when you're on holiday.
- You frequently work on weekends.
- You have holiday or personal days left at the end of the year.
- You have referred to yourself as a "workaholic."
- You wish you could spend more time doing things outside of work that you enjoy.
- You think overworking could be affecting your overall performance.

There are no easy answers. These statements are designed to cause a bit of self-reflection. Consider whether or not you're maintaining an appropriate work–life balance. We all know that working hard doesn't necessarily mean working smart. In Chapter 24, we provide you with some tips on how to free up time by having productive and efficient work habits. Delegating; focusing on priorities; managing paperwork, emails, and a calendar; and saying no on occasion—these all potentially lead to a less stressful and more productive workday.

It's true that hard work never killed anybody, but I figure, why take the chance?

–Ronald Reagan, Gridiron Club speech

Sharpened Focus

Understanding how to narrow one's energies and focus on what needs to get done is a characteristic of someone with emotional intelligence. People with high EI are able to channel energy, concentrate, and meet deadlines. They don't procrastinate or get lost in unimportant details.

This is something to think about if your Number 1 trait is open-minded. Open-minded types can often lack focus and become distracted because of their natural curiosity and imagination. The ability to concentrate tends to be easier for the head-driven personality. Setting goals and prioritizing activities can be helpful in harnessing energy and managing how time is spent.

Ability to Handle Stress

It's easy to ignore or become accustomed to how much stress you are under. People with high emotional intelligence are better able to manage their response to daily demands on their time and energy. People with different personality traits will react to stressful situations and manage stress differently:

- *Open-minded* people can become scattered and begin to visualize scenarios that will never happen.
- *Extroverted* people can lash out at people and blame them for whatever is going wrong.
- *Agreeable* people can withdraw, avoid confrontation, and hold in emotions.
- *Conscientious* people can become righteously self-indignant and psychologically rigid.
- *Emotionally stable* people can display coldness, meanness, and haughtiness.

Now that you understand your shadow, can you see why you react the way you do when you're under stress?

SOCIAL INTELLIGENCE

Social intelligence is about turning your marketplace ecosystem into your advocate. You want to coordinate actions that lead to positive outcomes by creating trust between and among people. People expand their relationship with you, refer business opportunities, and publicly advocate for you and your company. Social intelligence is essentially how emotional intelligence plays out in your ecosystem.

EMOTIONAL INTELLIGENCE AND PERSONALITY TRAITS

It should now be clear that your personality plays a role in your emotional intelligence. Some people are naturally more empathetic, balanced, calm, and introspective. Some people are naturally more disagreeable, quick to react, volatile, and emotional.

It's a growth step to accept that your personality strengths come with a corresponding shadow. It's not always easy, but people with high emotional intelligence better control their shadow behavior. They also do a better job of managing around their Number 5–ranked trait.

Leaders who exhibit high emotional intelligence are in big demand because they create a positive organizational culture. One of our favorite questions to ask our leadership coaching clients is, "Do you want to be the smartest person in the room, or the most mature person in the room?" When you develop an earned reputation for being the most mature person in the room, doors start opening. People begin to ask you to have a seat at the table.

The good news is that with applied energy and effort, you can improve and enhance your emotional intelligence, much more than your IQ. Each personality type exhibits maturity differently. No matter what your dominant personality trait is, the common denominator is that the more mature you are, the less you project your ego. Less ego projection translates into better listening skills and stronger objectivity in evaluating emotional dynamics. These behaviors are always sought after in the C-suite.

15 INTERDEPENDENT RESONANCE

Your workday is likely spent interfacing with dozens of people: direct reports, peers, senior leaders, and prospects or clients. Getting your business ecosystem to work for you is critical to your success. Establishing interdependent resonance and connecting in a meaningful way with everyone around you is key to becoming a strategic leader—being able to orchestrate human potential into dynamic transactional systems.

Think of someone you deeply resonate with. Your choice could be a friend, relative, spouse, boss, client, or coworker. You'll know who to choose by your level of empathy with and attunement to each other's physical and emotional states. We've all had a similar experience—when you haven't seen someone in years, yet 2 minutes after you meet, you're exactly where you left off. The passage of time didn't affect the relationship. This phenomenon occurs because your brains link and sync—they're actually lighting up in the same place (see Chapter 13).

Now consider why the two of you resonate. How do you rank this person's Big Five personality traits, and what is their Number 1–ranked trait? Open-minded people tend to connect with other open-minded people. Extroverts

https://doi.org/10.1037/0000391-016
Becoming a Strategic Leader: Capitalize on the Power of Your Personality, by G. W. Watts & L. Blazek

better connect with other extroverts—same with agreeable people. Conscientious people seek out others like them, as do emotionally stable people. We generally like people we perceive of as like ourselves. Birds of a feather do, in fact, flock together. But the opposite can also be true: People with opposite personalities—that is, the Number 1 trait of one is the same as the Number 4 or 5 trait of the other—are attracted because the relationship helps overcome the relative weaknesses of each. Relationships flourish when people's strengths and brands add value to each other.

People also resonate when they behave true to themselves. No one needs to role-play, except in circumstances in which a certain decorum is required. Authenticity and a sense of mutual trust, genuineness, respect, and empathy—this combination is what creates positive dynamics in interpersonal relationships. This is what creates interdependent resonance.

People resonate when they behave true to themselves.

ELEMENTS OF INTERDEPENDENT RESONANCE

The elements of interdependent resonance can be summarized as liking, empathy, commonality, self-disclosure, genuineness and authenticity, and positive energy. We'll discuss each of these elements in detail and the ways personality traits influence how they manifest.

Liking

It seems obvious, but genuine liking has to exist for resonance to occur. It's no secret that we tend to say yes to requests from people we know and like.

Let's identify some of the reasons we like someone. We like people

- who have common interests
- who flatter us and make us feel good about ourselves
- who feel familiar and comfortable
- who are positive and associated with good news
- who are easy to engage with
- who are physically attractive

Try to recall the last time you made a purchase or commitment based solely on someone's appearance or pleasant personality. Many studies have been done on this topic. There's no doubt that products and services are routinely sold on the basis of factors having nothing to do with their particular attributes. It's important to recognize this if you lead a business development team. In a competitive situation where all things are essentially equal, liking could be the determining factor in winning a piece of business.

Another issue, as it relates to liking, is unconscious bias. If you've ever made a bad hire, is it possible that you made the hiring decision based more on personality than on qualifications and competence? Do you have any "favorites" on your team? Is it possible you like them because they remind you of yourself? Be aware that liking and unconscious bias often play a role in the decisions you make every day.

If you're an introvert and less comfortable extending yourself into your environment, pay special attention to the power of liking. Strong performance and competence often are not enough to guarantee success in your next career move, particularly in circumstances when organizational changes are taking place. We don't need to tell you that companies today are trying to do more with less. If there are three people vying for two seats, don't lose out because you haven't focused on building relationships. One of the most important things you can do for your career is to develop a strong and supportive network within your organization. Make an extra effort to build genuine relationships. If you don't, you might be left out in the cold one day.

Understanding the power of liking doesn't mean you need to be unethical or disingenuous. Just realize that people generally prefer to say yes and will go the extra mile for people who they know and like, who are attractive, and who are like them. Positioning yourself to take advantage of this pattern of behavior is good not only for business, but for your career.

You may have heard of or read Dale Carnegie's classic book, published in 1936, *How to Make Friends and Influence People*. Carnegie's advice is simple, but not easy. Become genuinely interested in people—smile, encourage others to talk about themselves and their interests, and make them feel important. What, if anything, has changed since 1936? The answer is essentially nothing—except that we're now aware that the concept of resonance, as a result of liking someone, is neurologically based and completely real.

Think of liking as a building block, a foundation upon which you build your career. When people like you, your world gets a little better.

Empathy

Empathy is the ability to identify with the feelings of another person. Empathetic people are able to recognize and perceive the emotions of others. Sensing what someone is feeling is the essence of empathy. Being empathetic, or at least attempting to be empathetic, can reap big rewards. Showing empathy in a conversation can often improve the interpersonal dynamics. Being tuned into other people's feelings is no doubt easier for heart-driven personalities—they naturally "feel" others' emotions.

Watch out for common ego-based destroyers of empathy, such as interrupting to give advice, talking about your interests, or judging what's being said. If empathy doesn't come naturally to you, try once a day to make a conscious effort to respond to a comment with real empathy, and watch the response. See whether this improves the quality of your conversations and makes you feel more connected to the person you're speaking to. Never underestimate the beauty of being silent. Not jumping in to respond, give advice, or express your opinion can often be the most empathetic thing you can do.

You have a grand gift of silence, Watson. It makes you quite invaluable as a companion.

—Sir Arthur Conan Doyle, "The Man With the Twisted Lip"

Commonality

Commonality refers to the perception of how similar two people are. Simply put, people feel more comfortable with those who are like them or have something in common with them.

This advice may seem elementary, but find out what you have in common with others, especially when meeting someone new. When you indicate a sincere interest in the subjects and areas a person feels are important, barriers break down more quickly. Unconsciously, they begin to feel connected to you. The agreeable personality type tends to find commonality naturally. Once trust has been established (and this may take time), you can deepen the conversation by asking the person to discuss ideas, opinions, values, and beliefs. These are the strongest bonds of commonality.

There are many things you can learn about an individual, particularly one you have never met, through social media and the internet. As we mentioned previously, this due diligence takes very little time and should be routine preparation before any important conversation. Having insight into the background and interests of the individual you are meeting with will help you to quickly leverage common interests.

Self-Disclosure

Let's talk about talking about yourself. We're going to call talking about yourself *self-disclosure*. Self-disclosure is a necessary building block for intimacy—a feeling of closeness and connection in an interpersonal relationship. Intimacy simply cannot be achieved without genuine self-disclosure. We routinely disclose information about ourselves. The important question is, What's the right amount of self-disclosure?

In business, we expect self-disclosure to be reciprocal and appropriate. The sharing of personal or business information between people should be equal in emotional depth. This probably seems obvious, but we've all been in meetings where the level of self-disclosure only goes one way. If you share about yourself and the other person doesn't reciprocate, the subliminal message is that the other person is not emotionally connecting with you. Resonance isn't happening.

Most people will look for assurance regarding your intentions before they trust you with information about their business issues, problems, or even personal matters. The general effect of self-disclosure is to promote accepting trust behavior and reduce or eliminate defensive behavior. We suggest that you resist talking about yourself unless it's clearly relevant to the conversation. You'll almost always learn more by listening than by talking—especially about yourself.

Genuineness and Authenticity

Genuineness and authenticity have to do with being natural—being who you really are. It's about projecting honesty in all of your dealings. Your tone of voice, body language, and verbal expression should all be congruent with your natural personality. Being genuine and authentic is easier for the agreeable personality, who is naturally unguarded. When people perceive that you're holding back or role-playing, they often react by being defensive. It's because they don't trust the essence of who you're projecting yourself to be. Being an inauthentic leader can have a ripple effect, stifling open communication, trust, and collaboration.

You can be authentic regardless of your personality structure. Maturity is essentially lightening your ego-based shadows. Becoming mature means becoming authentic. When you're maturely authentic, you're less anxious and under less stress because you are being who you really are.

Positive Energy

We all want to be around people who are engaging. We're naturally drawn to those who radiate positive energy, who make others feel good just being in their presence. Emotionally intelligent leaders create positive energy. They're skilled at reading body language, mood, and tone of voice. They're not afraid to allow themselves to get close to others. Intimacy is established quickly and appropriately because such leaders are comfortable lowering their own defenses. Occasionally, they even point out flaws within themselves to connect on a more human level. They offer objective and genuine support because of their elevated ability to empathize. Being at ease with their emotions, they easily relate to others. People feel connected to a leader who can positively articulate their feelings.

Emotionally intelligent leaders create positive energy.

When you're energized, people will connect to your energy. Each personality type becomes energized when discussing topics and dynamics they intuitively understand and relate to. Here's how each personality type tends to energize discussions:

- *Open-minded* people energize others when discussing strategy, big ideas, and their vision for the future.

- *Extroverted* people energize others when discussing expanding business opportunities, introducing new contacts, and growing their sphere of influence.

- *Agreeable* people energize others when discussing creating and expanding partnering relationships.

- *Conscientious* people energize others when analyzing details and laying out a complex process.

- *Emotionally stable* people energize others when discussing how the merits of a product or service are measured and assessed for success.

RECAP OF INTERDEPENDENT RESONANCE

Don't underestimate the power of liking, empathy, commonality, self-disclosure, genuineness and authenticity, and positive energy. Together, these behaviors contribute to the very real concept of interdependent resonance. Remember, if a leader doesn't resonate with their team, the team is merely a group of people. Emotional maturity and mastery of these interpersonal skills are essential to becoming a strategic leader.

16 LISTENING

Are all great leaders great listeners? The answer is no. A LinkedIn survey of 14,000 employees by futurist Jacob Morgan found that only 8% considered their leaders to be great listeners and communicators.

One of the most successful leaders of the 20th century isn't well known for his listening skills. When Steve Jobs took his original Macintosh team on its first retreat, one member asked whether they should do some market research to see what customers wanted. "No," Jobs replied, "because customers don't know what they want until we've shown them."

Jobs's Number 1 personality trait was open-minded, and his Number 2 trait was conscientious. We believe that his two positive descriptors were "pioneering achiever," referring specifically to his pioneering design skills and relentless drive for achievement. Steve Jobs is an excellent example of how outlier traits can be leveraged for optimal success: They were perfectly aligned with the skills necessary to drive Apple's strategy.

In terms of his listening ability, we suspect that Jobs's shadow descriptors were "obsessive eccentric." His shadows were strong and very apparent. He had no need to fit in and didn't seek the approval of others. He believed

https://doi.org/10.1037/0000391-017
Becoming a Strategic Leader: Capitalize on the Power of Your Personality, by G. W. Watts & L. Blazek

obsessively in himself and his ideas. It wasn't in his go-to mindset to seek input. His selective listening skills were a reflection of his dominant shadow combination of obsessiveness and eccentricity.

The example of Steve Jobs is the exception. It's rare when listening isn't important to leadership success. Listening involves suspending judgment to understand and to seek out the opinions, ideas, and thinking of others. Listening with emotional maturity demonstrates mastery over emotional reactivity.

Listening is hard work. It takes patience, concentration, and being in the moment. Your ego is the part of your mind that seeks validation and recognition. Generally, the more you need to talk, the more your ego is "projecting," which is another way of saying "interfering." As we have stated, self-awareness is the most important aspect of becoming a better listener. When you know yourself well, you've already validated yourself to yourself. When you've acknowledged your own personality strengths and feel confident, you'll have less need to draw attention to yourself. You are more open to hearing what others have to say.

Self-awareness is the most important aspect of becoming a better listener.

HOW GOOD A LISTENER ARE YOU, REALLY?

How many of these apply to you? Be honest!

- I listen more than I speak.
- When listening, I am rarely thinking ahead to what I'm going to say next.
- I don't talk over people or interrupt.
- I focus entirely on what's being said and don't look at the time.
- I rarely jump ahead or finish the other person's thoughts.
- I don't bring up inconsistencies or errors in what's been said.
- I routinely ask open-ended questions like "Can you tell me more?"
- I often reflect back what the other person has said to be sure there's no miscommunication.
- I summarize at the end of conversations to be certain everyone's on the same page.

Being a good listener demonstrates respect for the person who is speaking. You'll generally be rewarded when you strive to listen. Listening allows you your right to speak.

> Listening allows you your right to speak.

You should set the example for what great listening looks and feels like. It's especially challenging listening to someone whose personality isn't the same as yours and when they're speaking language that resonates with them, and not you. You're not going to walk out of every meeting thinking, "Wow, that was a great conversation." But it's up to you to try and make each conversation better than it might have been before you understood the Big Five personality traits and the language that resonates best with each personality type.

THE MAGIC OF THE OPEN-ENDED QUESTION

Asking open-ended questions moves the conversation deeper and indicates to the speaker that you're interested and would like to hear more. Pay attention, and you'll begin to notice how few people actually follow up a statement with an open-ended question. Most people are in their own head, focused on what they're going to say next. It takes practice and effort to be completely in the moment and able to fully concentrate on what's being said. It's really about being emotionally mature and keeping your ego need for attention and recognition in check.

When you ask an open-ended question, you're validating the other person while helping expand the discussion. Open-ended questions typically begin with words such as "what" and "how," or phrases such as "Tell me about. . . ." When you follow up a statement with an open-ended question, you're sending a signal that you're engaged in the conversation. Unconscious barriers begin to break down. Even head-driven conscientious and emotionally stable types can feel more comfortable speaking genuinely and authentically. Sometimes they need to get out of their own way, but when they do, the conversation is every bit as meaningful as conversations with the other heart-driven personality types.

> When you ask an open-ended question, you're validating the other person while helping expand the discussion.

You'll know you're listening effectively when the other person remarks, often with genuine surprise, how long they've been talking. When you regularly listen this well, you'll discover something important—how to truly be in the moment and focus on someone else. When you ask the right question and the other person is surprised by the lucidity of their own answer, you're providing an "Aha!" experience. Their answer taught them something, and that something was their own insight. This experience is akin to Socratic questioning. Socratic questioning adds value by helping others explore complex situations, uncover poor or biased thinking, and identify issues and problems. People begin to distinguish what they know from what they need to know.

You know you're listening effectively when the other person remarks, with genuine surprise, how long they've been talking.

Who do you think is the best interviewer on television? We recommend that you watch or listen to a variety of interviewers. Observe the number of open-ended questions they ask and how the conversation with the interviewee moves back and forth. Notice what percentage of time the interviewer is talking. Also notice when an interview flows seamlessly and effortlessly. When an interview stalls, can you make out what happened or what went wrong?

When you encourage thinking but challenge it and ask questions nobody else is asking, you bring out the best in people. Here are some examples of open-ended questions that tap into people's insights:

- To clarify thinking: "Can you share more of your thinking?"
- To challenge thinking: "What are the factors that drive this perspective?"
- To provide evidence: "What causes you to hold that viewpoint?"
- To consider alternative viewpoints: "How do we make sure we include all perspectives?"
- When all else fails: "Is there anything else?" or "Can you tell me more?"

These open-ended questions and their ability to garner information will yield more engaging conversations and deeper relationships. As you become more conscious of using open-ended questions, notice what happens to the interpersonal dynamics. Pay attention to identify when asking that one additional question made a huge difference in the quality of information exchanged in the conversation.

View meetings with direct reports, clients, and other professionals as an opportunity to observe the quality of the interpersonal exchange. Notice when great questions are asked and when someone missed an easy opportunity to ask that perfect open-ended or follow-up question. Meetings provide an opening for you to coach others on the power of asking the question no one else had thought to ask.

Think back to when someone you respected asked you a question that caused you to think or reflect upon a set of circumstances in a whole new way. How did your perception of that person change as a result?

REFLECTIVE LISTENING

Reflective listening is taking what is said and restating it with brevity and conciseness. Occasionally summarizing thoughts and ideas to make sure you are following is almost always a good idea. Clarify and restate what's being said. When you excel at this skill, you'll increase your ability to understand the message being delivered. It also helps the other person clarify their own thinking. Reflecting isn't asking questions or telling someone how they feel, what they believe, or what they want; reflecting is summarizing what you're being told, making sure you understand, and confirming you understand.

Business professionals know that listening is hard work. They'll often acknowledge and give you credit for your effort. When someone is trying hard to listen and you sense it, doesn't that increase your respect for the person? It's likely you're reciprocating that feeling of respect because you believe they're showing respect to you.

LISTENING TIPS

If you focus on three things, you'll notice an improvement in the quality of your conversations:

1. Listen more than you speak.
2. Use open-ended questions to gain additional information and expand the discussion.
3. Summarize what is being said so that you can be sure everyone is on the same page.

17 LISTENING AND BODY LANGUAGE EXERCISES

Oddly enough, the more people talk, the better listeners they perceive themselves to be. They enjoy listening to themselves and unconsciously think, "Gee, I'm enjoying listening to myself; therefore, I must be a great listener!" This is a sign of low self-awareness.

We've said this before, but it bears repeating: People like and appreciate being listened to. When you listen carefully, you validate the person speaking. Defense barriers break down and self-esteem increases; they feel valued and respected. Listening isn't easy. If it were, everyone would be good at it.

Professional training in listening skills and body language observation is increasing in acceptance and popularity. For example, businesses across a wide spectrum are putting high performers through intensive improvisation training to improve their listening skills. In this chapter, we share some simple yet impactful techniques for sharpening your skills and observations.

LISTENING EXERCISES

We recommend two listening exercises: One is the "yes, and . . ." technique, and the other is a summarizing exercise.

https://doi.org/10.1037/0000391-018
Becoming a Strategic Leader: Capitalize on the Power of Your Personality, by G. W. Watts & L. Blazek

"Yes, and . . ." Technique

Improvisational comedy has been around for several thousand years. The art form is believed to have started in ancient Greece. *Improvisation* is a spontaneous reaction in the moment and in response to the environment. You're improvising every day—listening and spontaneously reacting to what others say and what the environment dictates.

A fundamental technique taught in every basic improvisation class is called "Yes, and. . . ." This technique compels you to listen intently and then positively build upon what's being said. Saying "Yes, and . . ." is about accepting what the other person has to offer in order to draw them into the scene. The "Yes, and . . ." technique gives you the chance to acknowledge what's been said, and then move the conversation to a new place where you just might discover something new and interesting.

"Yes and . . ." accelerates the conversation into new territory where unlimited possibilities exist. The idea is that one person offers a thought, idea, or statement and the other person accepts the offer with "Yes," and then begins to expand upon it with "and." This exercise teaches people to accept statements made by their fellow players.

It may seem silly, but it's not when you really think about it. We've all been in meetings where someone corrected or disagreed with a colleague or client, halting the momentum of the discussion. Saying "Yes, and . . ." builds communication and creates positive energy. Seek value in what's being said. Agree, and then contribute further by adding a new dimension.

I recently used this technique with a CEO. Over the phone I gave a "Yes," and then tried to add to it. The CEO responded, and I followed up his response with another "Yes, and. . . ." Initially, the CEO told me he only had a quick minute. We hung up 30 minutes later after a conversation that moved our relationship forward. All I did, in the most authentic way, was say "Yes, and . . .," and then build on his statement so he could respond from a higher place.

Your goal should be to constantly elevate a discussion. As the conversation deepens, the positive feelings that result will now be associated with you.

Your goal should be to constantly elevate a discussion.

In your next conversation, try using "Yes, and . . ." as often as you can. This is naturally going to be easier for people with the agreeable personality trait, but give it a try. You'll be surprised at how positively this simple verbal reinforcement will play out in real life.

When we were creating our audio book, we were in the recording studio for many hours. The technicians were obviously listening to the content of the book and were editing the recording after each session. Following the recording of the section on listening skills, which included the "yes, and . . ." technique, one of the technicians told us a personal story. On the evening of our last session, he went home and began using "yes, and . . ." with his wife. He said he was amazed with what happened. By using this simple technique, he quickly created positive energy and sent the signal to his wife that he was really listening and engaged in the conversation. This, he explained, set the tone for a very pleasant evening at home.

Clearly, the technique of "yes, and . . ." has broad applications! But the bottom line is that it forces you to listen well and then positively build on what's being said. It also sends a message to the other person that you're listening. How can this be a bad thing? It's worth the effort to practice using this technique. You'll see for yourself what a simple but effective tool it is.

Take note, however, that if someone uses "Yes, *but* . . ." the conversation will quickly become negative. "Yes, but . . ." is really like "no." It's a killer on several levels. If emotional stability is your Number 1 personality trait, you likely have a propensity to judge and critique. Pay attention. You may not even be aware that saying "yes, but . . ." is something you routinely do.

If you can, attend a live improvisation performance. If this isn't an option, go online and watch a few segments of any comedy improvisation show. In improvisation, players are given random topics and asked to create a scene. Pay attention to the rhythm between the participants and the flow of the dialogue. Listen for the "Yes, and . . ." pattern. It takes incredible listening skills and focus to do this well, and even greater skill to be funny while doing it.

Summarizing Exercise

Find a partner; virtually anybody will do. Ask this person to talk for 90 seconds about the frustrations in their job. Put your watch on the table between the two of you. Tell your partner that once they stop talking, you'll summarize what's been said. You're going to try and distill their core message into one sentence.

What was this experience like for you? Were you able to summarize what was said in just one sentence? Was it hard to avoid speaking during the exercise? Were you surprised at how much you wanted to talk? After you stated that your goal was to summarize, did you notice how much more intensely you listened? When you can do this consistently, you're on the path to becoming a better listener.

This exercise will help you become aware of how disciplined you are in controlling your urge to speak. It also demonstrates that when you agree to summarize, you're likely to pay extra attention to what's being said. Try this exercise when you're on the phone or in a meeting. Silently tell yourself to listen as long as possible; speak only to ask a question or to summarize, making sure that you heard correctly. You'll appreciate this simple, powerful growth step.

BODY LANGUAGE EXERCISES

Effective exercises that can improve your ability to read body language include behavior observations and mimicking body language.

Behavior Observations

There are a couple of additional exercises you can try when you're out in your environment. The idea is to increase your awareness of how different personality types behave.

When you're in a restaurant or coffee shop, take a few minutes to look around the room. See what personality traits you can identify just by how people express themselves using their bodies. The purpose of this exercise is to focus on your environment and become comfortable assessing people's personality based on what you are observing.

Observe three strangers and try to identify their top personality trait. Here are some pointers:

- *Open-minded:* Open-minded people actively use their imagination, often leaning their head against their hand or looking up and away as if they're visualizing. They can have difficulty staying in the moment, so they'll appear as if they're thinking about something or someplace other than where they are.

- *Extroverted:* Extroverted people use energy and enthusiasm to demonstrate how they're feeling. Are they expressive? Do they use hand gestures? Do they spread themselves out, showing that they enjoy taking up space?

- *Agreeable:* Agreeable people use their body language to suggest a genuine interest in people. Does the person naturally touch people around them or help out by collecting menus or pouring water? Are they smiling sincerely and focusing intently on others?

- *Conscientious:* Conscientious people arrange or adjust things on the table. Do they take out a notebook and start writing? Do they straighten their silverware or separate the servings on the plate, keeping them from touching each other?

- *Emotionally stable:* Emotionally stable people seem calm while using self-monitoring, for example, by crossing their arms maintaining a firm, vertical stance or posture. Does the person appear serious and show minimal body language?

Mimicking Body Language

When you are sitting across from someone, observe and then mimic their body language. If they cross their legs, you do it, too. Hold your head at the same angle. You can do this exercise in a bar, restaurant, or at a social gathering. Feel free to practice this at home, too.

The purpose of this exercise is to increase your powers of observation and empathy. People with heart-driven personality traits will more naturally be sensitive to the feelings of others. What happened when you mimicked the other's body language? Did you feel any of the emotions of the person you were imitating? Did you consciously feel any change in the energy between the two of you?

People continuously communicate through their body language, so be observant. Does the person lean back, pulling away from the energy to maintain their objectivity? Do they cross their arms? Do they lean in, wanting to become a part of the combined energy? Do they express themselves by using gestures? What does their body language reveal about their dominant personality trait, or about how they are unconsciously feeling about the interpersonal dynamic?

WORK TO BECOME A GREAT LISTENER

We attempted to make the "Yes, and . . ." and body language exercises fun and interesting. However, do not confuse "fun and interesting" with "trivial and elementary." Firms like Citibank send people to improvisation training at Chicago's Second City for a reason. The second author attended Second City when at Citibank and found this training to be extremely valuable. Organizations know that they're going to win more deals and make more money if their professionals understand how to quickly react in the moment, build on what a client is saying and feeling, and recognize the meaning behind unconscious body language. We recommend that you practice these listening and body language exercises and see what happens.

18 HOW TO INFLUENCE BEHAVIOR

Every interaction has consequences. Even the simplest conversations can have a profound impact somewhere down the road. As a leader, you want people on your team—metaphorically speaking. In other words, you want to be able to influence people to buy into you and your ideas. It can be surprisingly easy to exert influence on others, which is why we recommend that you read and study the book *Influence: Science and Practice,* by Robert Cialdini. He's discovered several patterns of behavior that are so powerful we believe they deserve discussion here.

To some degree, we all use and fall victim to what Cialdini brilliantly labels "weapons of influence" in our daily interactions. We can become skilled at using these concepts and ethically putting them into practice.

It makes sense that people are more likely to process and respond to information effectively when they have both the desire and the ability to analyze that information carefully. But time is valuable, and people often use what Cialdini calls the "click–whirr response," or fixed-action patterns of behavior. The "click" is the tape being activated, and the "whirr" is the rollout of a standard sequence of behaviors.

https://doi.org/10.1037/0000391-019
Becoming a Strategic Leader: Capitalize on the Power of Your Personality, by G. W. Watts & L. Blazek

Scientists have discovered a number of mental shortcuts we all use when making everyday decisions. These shortcuts—for example, "if it's expensive, it must be good" or "if an expert said so, it must be true"—no doubt simplify our thinking and save time. This works well most of the time but can leave us exposed to costly mistakes. We need decision-making shortcuts to deal with the enormous amount of information we're processing every day. Although shortcuts are necessary, we can lose accurate thinking when making decisions using shortcuts. You might expect that professionals in a business setting would be less likely to use such shortcuts, but surprisingly, that's not the case.

Influencing techniques can be used ethically in all phases of the transaction cycle. As we study these concepts in detail, consider how to apply each in your day-to-day dealings. If you practice using them and pay attention to their effectiveness, you'll understand how powerful they are.

RECIPROCITY

Most people are familiar with the concept of reciprocity. The principle of reciprocity manifests itself in all relationships. Reciprocity means that when you extend energy for somebody, they feel a psychological need to repay you—to even the score. It's been scientifically proven that doing someone a favor causes them to feel compelled to reciprocate. Interestingly, the recipient of the favor often reciprocates by performing an even greater favor than the initial one. Think about the implications of this: Even a small gesture can potentially alter the balance of power and increase the probability of a positive or even greater response.

The principle of reciprocity manifests itself in all relationships.

All of the Big Five personality traits have a need to balance energy. Regardless of how a person's traits are ranked, there's a need to balance energy. Think about a time you felt you owed someone because they'd done you a special favor. Wasn't that a powerful motivator for you to act in a certain way? Think about a time someone demonstrated reciprocity for something you had done, whether a favor, action, or perceived concession. How did their act of reciprocity make you feel about the person?

Reciprocity can manifest in a variety of ways. An example you may not have considered is a request for you to present your position or perspective. It's likely that a client or colleague will do so because they feel they've been heard and now want to hear from you. Maybe a question you asked sparked a desire to listen further and discuss a topic more deeply. Because you've listened well, they now want to reward you with the reciprocal action of listening to you.

Early on, we're taught that favors are special and should be returned. This is a social norm that causes most of us to take reciprocal action.

Developing reciprocal relationships with clients, gatekeepers, colleagues, and centers of influence can yield exceptional results. An obligation to repay a favor exists only because one has chosen to receive from others. By receiving something of perceived value from you, the recipient now feels indebted, and the power dynamic has shifted, even if only on the unconscious level. Most of us find it uncomfortable or agitating to be in a state of obligation; agreeable people, in particular, place a high value on maintaining harmonious relationships and quickly seek to restore balance. But the rest of us don't like the feeling of being beholden, either. For this reason, when an imbalance results, the recipient of a favor will often agree to perform a larger favor than they received.

Reciprocal concessions are an example of how reciprocity can be used in negotiation or in "selling" your ideas or positions. Presenting a request in a way that exploits the power of reciprocity is a surprisingly effective way to increase the likelihood of a positive outcome. First, make a large request that you consider likely be turned down. Once the initial request is declined, make a lesser request, which is the one you were really interested in. It's very difficult for someone to turn you down twice, especially when the second request is smaller than the first.

There are many ways to ethically use reciprocity in business. Be aware of opportunities to do small acts of kindness for people who are in a position to help you down the road. Simple things like forwarding useful articles of interest, making an extra effort to accommodate someone's busy schedule, or sending a handwritten thank you note can pay off in a big way. When someone cancels a meeting at the last minute, this may be an opportunity for you to capitalize on their feeling of indebtedness. Listen for clues about any personal issues that are important. If you walk into a client's or colleague's office and they're selling their child's fundraising candy, buy some. The weapon of reciprocity will increase the odds that your money is well spent.

COMMITMENT AND CONSISTENCY

Studies have shown a very strong connection between commitment and consistency. Consistency is underestimated but often is formidable in directing human action and behavior. It's a highly valued quality, equated with trustworthiness and dependability. If I can get you to make a commitment, there's a higher probability you'll comply because you feel an unconscious pressure to be consistent. According to Cialdini, understanding the relationship between commitment and consistency is a powerful weapon of influence.

Much research has been published about the committing power of written statements. It's good practice to ask someone to memorialize their commitment by writing it down. This activity is a powerful way to make someone feel more psychologically connected to what they've promised. Recording something on paper is tangible evidence of commitment that makes it feel real for both parties.

Recording something on paper is tangible evidence of commitment that makes it feel real for both parties.

Although not as powerful as a written commitment, a verbal commitment is a close second. Once they have made a verbal commitment, most people will act with consistency. Verbal commitments are especially effective when they're made in public and viewed as completely voluntary. The more people there are in the room when the verbal commitment is made, the more difficult it will be to renege.

A classic example of the effect of a public verbal commitment that wasn't followed by consistency is a statement made by George H. W. Bush at the Republican Convention in 1988. His declaration, "Read my lips: no new taxes" was followed by tax increases during his term as president. Although the reason for the tax increases might have been legitimate, the fact that the public declaration had been made was overriding. Taped footage of this declaration was used in a devastating attack ad by Bill Clinton's campaign in 1992. It is widely believed that this ad contributed significantly to Bush losing his reelection bid.

People whose Number 1– or 2–ranked personality traits are emotionally stable and conscientious place more value on commitment and consistency. They live in a world of rationality and facts. They are likely to act consistent with what they've done before, even if the situation is completely different and the prior action was a mistake. There's a perception of safety and order in consistency. If you obtain a written or verbal commitment from someone with a head-driven personality, there's a good chance they'll follow through and do what they say they're going to do.

Watch out, however, for commitments made by someone who falls on the heart-driven side of our model, especially strong extroverts. Extroverts live in the present and place a high value on their real-time positive interaction with others. Consequently, they are predisposed to agree to requests but are often inconsistent in following through on commitments, particularly commitments that are verbal. Extroverts can make good-faith promises that they ultimately never keep.

SOCIAL PROOF

Most people don't like to be viewed as outliers. Our behavior often reflects an unconscious need to validate our ideas, beliefs, and actions against the ideas, beliefs, and actions of others. Social proof is the concept that the more people we find who believe our idea is correct, the more strongly we perceive the idea to be correct. Pay attention to how many people are swayed by disinformation. If they believe that a source is credible and that a large number of people accept what is being said as true, they'll jump on board.

In a business context, we see the demonstration of social proof in advertisements claiming large numbers of users of a particular product or service. It's human nature for consumers to look to the behavior and buying patterns of others to justify our own behavior. That's why endorsements are so frequently used in advertisements. The tendency to copy what others are doing is a common way of making purchasing decisions. When we're unsure of ourselves, we're even more apt to put faith in the decisions of others, especially when those people seem just like us.

Social proof is most effective under two conditions. The first is uncertainty: When people are unsure or the situation is ambiguous, they're more likely to accept the actions of others as correct. The second condition is similarity: People are more inclined to follow the lead of similar individuals. Although we do not advocate that the actions of others form the sole basis for decisions, we acknowledge social proof as a potent weapon of influence that can be used effectively in business. It really is true—monkey see, monkey do.

Social proof is most effective under two conditions:
uncertainty and similarity.

People look to the behavior of others for cues on how to behave. Herd behavior doesn't mean correct behavior, however. Just remember, there exists heavy social influence to copy what others are doing, especially when it seems that everyone is doing it.

AUTHORITY

There's strong pressure in most societies to comply with the requests of an authority. Authorities are assumed to possess superior levels of knowledge, wisdom, and power. Deference to authority is a good example of an automatic decision-making shortcut. When you actively demonstrate expertise or highly specialized knowledge, you're positioning yourself as an authority. When you're viewed as having a high degree of authority and expertise, people will unconsciously begin aligning with you.

Why do commercials use authority figures like doctors and celebrities to sell products and services? Most people don't stop to ask themselves whether someone who is professing to be an authority actually knows what they're talking about. Their demeanor, confidence, and trustworthiness are enough to convey authority status. Even your clothes and jewelry, the car you drive, the area you live in: We unconsciously use these things to judge your authority status. Remember, once you're perceived as an authority, you're almost always going to be considered an expert.

When using your personality strengths advantageously, it's easier for you to become an authority. You need education, training, and experience to build up competencies. But by channeling your competencies to your strengths, you'll enjoy the acquisition of new thinking and become an authority more quickly. You'll enjoy the learning because it's natural and intuitive.

By channeling your competencies to your strengths, you'll become an authority more quickly.

Open-minded people will want to brand themselves as an authority with respect to innovative experimentation and creative ideas. Extroverted people will want to become an authority on how to present and expand contacts and business opportunities. Agreeable people will want to be an authority on the deepening of relationships and the creation of collaborative teams. Conscientious people will want to become an authority on process and efficiency. Emotionally stable types will want to be an authority on objectively evaluating outcomes using quantifiable data.

Understand that if you and your company truly have credentials and highly specialized knowledge, you should position yourself to capitalize on this expertise. This is especially true when there is social proof to support your position as an expert in the marketplace.

SCARCITY AND THREAT OF LOSS

Why on earth would anyone in their right mind line up outside of a store for hours waiting for it to open? Only one answer makes sense: because they believe there's something inside the store that's valuable and of limited quantity. Opportunities always seem more valuable when they're less available, especially when there's competition for them. The longer the line, the greater the reinforcement that this behavior will result in obtaining something scarce and desirable.

Scarcity can be applied in a variety of contexts. Limiting access to a message causes individuals to want to receive it more and to become more favorable toward it. Limiting your availability can lead to the perception that because access to you is scarce, you are extremely busy and your product or service must therefore be highly desirable.

How many times have you tried to make an appointment, only to be told that they can't see you for weeks, or even months, from the date you call? First, you're annoyed, but almost automatically you find yourself believing that this professional must be very skilled and highly desirable if they're booked so far in advance.

Cialdini writes about the tactic toy companies use around the holidays of limiting the availability of "hot" toys. A parent might initially promise the hot toy to their child, but when that toy is unavailable, a parent has no choice but to purchase substitutes, often in greater quantity to make up for the disappointment. This is an effective way to increase sales in January when the hot toy suddenly becomes available again.

Behavioral science studies are clear—human beings are more motivated by the threat of loss than by the anticipation of gain. If you think you're going to lose something, especially something you perceive you already have, you're more fearful of losing it, which creates more anxiety than the anticipation of winning. We've all taken some action simply because we thought we had something to lose.

Human beings are more motivated by the threat of loss than by the anticipation of gain.

This powerful phenomenon exists in all cultures. It drives even the most rational people to behave in ways that seem counterintuitive, or even irrational. At the worst moments of the U.S. stock market crash of 2009, many fearful investors sold their holdings because they were afraid the market would continue to decline. For these people, the threat of further loss was simply overwhelming. It drove them to act irrationally, even contrary to the advice of their financial advisers.

So how can scarcity and threat of loss be applied to selling yourself and your ideas—in other words, to influencing and persuading? Most sales training encourages people to emphasize the benefits of the product or service they are selling. We don't disagree that emphasizing benefits is important; what we are suggesting is that under the right circumstances, creating agitation through the threat of loss might be an appropriate tool to use. Might a client be more inclined to make a buying decision if they knew that the resources necessary to solve their problem would be available only for a short time? Would they be more motivated to buy if they believed that the necessary variables (including time) were in limited supply? Would you be more likely to obtain approval for an initiative or project if you were able to articulate the negative consequences that could result from nonaction?

We're not suggesting that you create an illusion of scarcity or threat of loss where it doesn't exist. But when it's appropriate, scarcity and the threat of loss are highly motivating tools. In Chapter 20, we'll discuss how to apply the subtle threat of loss to your electronic communications. Just be aware that emphasizing what someone could lose can often be a more effective motivator than touting benefits.

Emphasizing what someone could lose can often be a more effective motivator than touting benefits.

INFLUENCING BEHAVIOR

The weapons of influence—reciprocity, commitment and consistency, social proof, authority, and scarcity and threat of loss—can all be used ethically and effectively in business. We encourage you to read *Influence: Science and Practice,* by Robert Cialdini, and to consider how to best leverage these powerful human dynamics.

19 PRESENTATION POINTERS

You're presenting in a variety of settings every day. Whether in a boardroom or a weekly staff meeting, the way you communicate matters. Even the most dynamic presenter won't resonate with an audience unless two factors are present.

First, before presenting your thoughts and ideas, you must have listened well and understood the salient issues and facts. Asking open-ended questions, using reflective listening, and summarizing what's been said are invaluable. It's a mistake to present your thoughts or solutions before you fully understand the situation.

It's a mistake to present your thoughts or solutions before you fully understand the situation.

Second, you'll want to engage others in what you're saying by creating an "Aha!" moment and using language that connects with all audience members' Number 1 personality trait.

https://doi.org/10.1037/0000391-020
Becoming a Strategic Leader: Capitalize on the Power of Your Personality, by G. W. Watts & L. Blazek

PRESENTING AND THE "AHA!"

What goes into a great presentation? The goal of a great presentation is for the audience to experience the golden moment of the "Aha!" The Aha! is a sudden realization, inspiration, insight, recognition, or comprehension. It can result from a proposal, solution, or a suggestion. Whatever the circumstances, your audience captures this insight and stores it in the brain. The Aha! is now a lasting impression in each person's memory. The impression is rewarding and pleasurable.

What's most interesting about this phenomenon is that when the audience experiences the Aha! their perception of you is instantly shifted in your favor. This moment is marked by a surge of electrical activity in the brain. In essence, the amygdala lights up; this is the part of the brain that attaches special weight to emotional events. When the amygdala is activated, audience members will remember your presentation long after it ends, and the memory will remain enjoyable. You're now associated with this pleasurable emotion and instantly regarded differently. If you've ever been in an engaging presentation that caused you to think differently, you know exactly how it feels. People want to follow a leader who is an inspiring presenter.

PRESENTING TO PEOPLE WITH EACH OF THE BIG FIVE PERSONALITY TRAITS

People with a given Number 1 personality trait perceive reality differently from those with the other Number 1 traits. It's just a fact. You can say the exact same thing, and each of the five personality types will interpret what you said differently. You've no doubt been in conversations in which you felt misunderstood or clearly misunderstood others. One reason for this could simply be poor listening skills. It's also possible, however, that these misunderstandings are the result of how each personality type processes information.

It's not always easy to be both heard and understood. We don't have to tell you how important this is to leaders. For this reason, we've spent a lot of time analyzing listening skills, identifying personality traits, and understanding what language connects with each trait.

Here are a few topics that relate to audience members with each dominant personality trait:

- *Open-minded:* Present strategy, describe the big picture, and visualize new ideas. Tie your discussion to a big question or statement.

- *Extroverted:* Present customer, market, and business expansion. Extroverts will connect to material they find energizing and exciting.

- *Agreeable:* Present in terms of partnering, deepening communication, strengthening company culture, and improving collaboration. Your discussion must build an emotional bond to connect with agreeable people.

- *Conscientious:* Present process, timeline expectations, commitment to quality, and follow-through. Conscientious people will identify with detail, delivery, and execution language.

- *Emotionally stable:* Present metrics and facts, and relate the past to the future. Emotionally stable people connect with rationality and measurement of results.

HOBBIES PROVIDE CLUES TO DOMINANT TRAITS

It can sometimes be difficult to rank a person's Big Five personality traits. Everyone has each of the Big Five traits embedded in their personality. Even if you're having trouble ranking a person's personality traits, the ranking still exists.

Even if you're having trouble ranking a person's personality traits, the ranking still exists.

I once consulted for a human capital company with a very effective CEO. She has since retired, leaving behind a satisfied and grateful board of directors. The rank-and-file admired her, too. By any definition, she was a real success. I remember how high functioning she was. She was creative, emotionally intelligent, hardworking, and always honest and objective in her relationships.

It was hard to tell what her Big Five ranking was because she was so high on each trait. It became clearer when I asked her what she did on a recent vacation. She told me she had a great time remodeling her daughter's bathroom. She did most of the work, with the exception of the electrical wiring. She enjoyed visualizing the design, and then she shared something revealing. She told me, "I designed the bathroom, fusing several archetypal themes together to get the feeling 'serene.'"

I thought, what kind of person would say something like that? Her Number 1 trait was open-minded; she was the kind of person who would tie design to archetypes. Another clue was that she designed the bathroom, did the remodeling work herself, and enjoyed the process. Her Number 2 trait was probably conscientious; she liked to execute the process that she had visualized.

Then an "Aha!" moment revealed to me how to present to her. She was a creative type who liked to visualize, but she also needed a process. I tailored our firm's presentation to reflect what I had discovered about her. I wanted a few PowerPoint slides to look "visionary" (one of the descriptors for open-minded; see Chapter 7), so I hired a creative artist. To appeal to her Number 2 trait of conscientious, we put in a follow-up slide labeled "Deliverables." I also made sure that our solution manifested and reflected her vision, which was easy to find in the annual chairman's letter, interviews, and LinkedIn profile.

Even though this CEO was hard to rank because she was so high on each trait, she still had a ranking—a ranking that was revealed by what she loved to do when she had free time. This told me who she really was.

Find out what someone likes to do in their spare time. In our spare time, we do what we like to do. The reason that we like it is because we enjoy the activity and are good at it, or trying to be. It captures our interest because it's aligned with our strengths. So, if you can, find out the hobbies or outside interests of the person you are presenting to, and then attempt to infer their personality type from the reasons they engage in the activity. For example, if someone loves to golf, the question is, Why do they love to golf?

- If they love to travel and enjoy new cultures and golf experiences, could this be a sign of open-mindedness?

- Some people like belonging to the country club more than the actual sport of golf because of the social aspects. So, is this an indication of that person being an extrovert?

- If they golf with the same people each week, could this be a clue that you're dealing with an agreeable person who values maintaining the relationships they've developed on the course?

- If they golf at the same time and same club every week, and have strong patterns of behavior they like to stick to, could this be a sign of conscientiousness?

- If they enjoy the finer technical points of the game and are constantly looking to improve, could this be an indicator of emotional stability?

The simple observation that a person likes golf isn't truly useful until you uncover what the person actually likes about golf. Asking open-ended questions to learn why someone likes golf will give you insight into their personality.

Some hobbies have a more obvious connection to a personality trait, however. For example, if someone is into cycling or gardening, it's likely that extroverted would be their Number 4– or 5–ranked trait. These are typically solitary activities and would be naturally appealing to someone who doesn't need to be around a lot of people.

Other hobbies can provide clues to someone's dominant personality trait. Does a person love to plan a trip down to minute details? If so, they might be conscientious. If they especially enjoy modern art, could they be open-minded? If they like to go to big events or parties, might they be extroverted? No one observation is generally enough. By making multiple observations over time, you will begin to identify a pattern.

With a little practice, you'll become more keenly aware of your environment and more comfortable examining behavior and ascribing personality traits. By using the Big Five classification system to categorize and analyze behavior, you can tailor your presentations and conversations to better connect with your audience.

FORMAL PRESENTATIONS TO A LARGER AUDIENCE

You may find yourself presenting in a boardroom setting or to a large audience. In these situations, it's challenging to understand which personality type to appeal to. A basic rule of thumb is to identify the decision-maker or the person with the most power, and then mold the presentation around them. Asking open-ended questions during a presentation and listening for clues in the answers can also help you to spontaneously adjust your language so that it connects with the personality type of the decision-maker or influencers.

Under ambiguous circumstances, you might consider creating a slide or talking points for each personality type.

- *Open-minded:* Emphasize future strategy and vision.
- *Extroverted:* Highlight growth, marketing, sales, or engagement.
- *Agreeable:* Discuss partnering, teamwork, and collaboration.
- *Conscientious:* Emphasize detail, process, and timelines.
- *Emotionally stable:* Illustrate metrics and projected results.

It may also help to determine the most probable dominant strain that runs through the culture of the company or business unit:

- Marketing and advertising tend to have an open-minded culture.
- Business development tends to have an extroverted culture.

- Customer service, internal consulting roles, and people who bridge internal and external boundaries are likely to have an agreeable culture.
- Accounting, data processing, delivery, and human resources are likely to have a conscientious culture.
- Finance, operations, quality control, and compliance tend to have an emotionally stable culture.

If you are presenting to an advertising or marketing firm, you can at least initially assume that open-minded is an important, and probably the prevailing, trait of the audience. Here you would include conceptual and creative ideas. If you are presenting to an audience in an accounting firm, you can initially assume that conscientious is the prevailing trait. Here you would include topics such as data analysis, process, and execution. Although we believe it's a good idea to have your presentations reflect the personality traits and ethos of the audience, please consider these rules of thumb to be generalizations and rough stereotypes.

WHEN PRESENTING, PERSONALITY OVERCOMES GENDER

Much has been written and discussed about the differences between men and women in business. Even journals like *Harvard Business Review* contain articles contrasting women's and men's buying behaviors. When men are pitching to women, they're often advised to be sensitive and to alter their pitch because women supposedly think, feel, and behave differently from men. But is this really accurate thinking?

Large-scale personality research has shown women to be slightly more agreeable and nurturing than men, and men to exhibit slightly more dominance. But this body of research is clear that differences in how the genders behave are only slight.

Personality differences are considerably more important in predicting behavior than gender. Think about it. Don't professional extroverted men and extroverted women act mostly identically in how they present themselves in the workplace? What's the real difference in job performance between a conscientious woman and a conscientious man? Does an emotionally stable male business analyst think and act differently than his female counterpart? The answer is no. Although popular culture might lead you to believe that men are from one planet and women are from another, gender disparities, particularly in business settings, are not nearly as important as personality.

> Personality differences are considerably more important in predicting behavior than gender.

PASSION

The goal of a presentation is to inspire and engage the audience. World-class presenters are passionate storytellers. Passionate storytelling involves a combination of heightened emotions, vivid language, expressive gestures, and engaging speech patterns. It aims to connect with the listener, convey the speaker's energy and enthusiasm, and create a memorable experience. People emotionally resonate and connect with mature passion.

> As a presenter, you must be a passionate storyteller.

If you believe your presentations lack passion, energy, and stage presence, we suggest that you invest in yourself. Hire a presentation skills coach. Former newscasters, announcers, and public relations professionals make excellent coaches. With a little practice, most people can become more confident and improve their ability to connect with an audience.

ENGAGING WITH YOUR AUDIENCE

Many presentation coaches emphasize the importance of appearance, physical gestures, and vocal presence. There are statistics supporting the claim that what you say isn't nearly as important as how you move and look and your tone of voice. We don't disagree that these factors are important in how your presentation is received. But isn't the purpose of a presentation to convey a message that is heard? Imagine how much more effective your presentations will be if you speak in language that actually resonates and connects with your audience.

20 CALL TO ACTION EMAILS

Emails and electronic communication are here to stay. The question is, How do you write an email that catches the reader's attention and causes them to take action based on the power of your message?

We believe that effective emails have three parts. Each part is critical. Reduce your emails to three sections that address each of the following:

- Part 1: Connect psychologically and create resonance.
- Part 2: Create anxiety by illustrating the consequence of doing nothing.
- Part 3: Issue the call to action.

This three-part email format is incredibly powerful. We use this simple yet highly effective format in our own coaching work. It can be used in any situation in which you're looking for someone to take action on your behalf. The sections that follow provide wording examples for each of the three parts.

https://doi.org/10.1037/0000391-021
Becoming a Strategic Leader: Capitalize on the Power of Your Personality, by G. W. Watts & L. Blazek

EMAIL PART 1: CONNECT PSYCHOLOGICALLY AND CREATE RESONANCE

Always open your email by appealing to the recipient's Number 1 trait. Doing this will begin to establish resonance. These five examples address each personality type:

- *Open-minded:* Thank you for our conversation. I appreciate your imaginative, "future vision" perspective.

- *Extroverted:* Thank you for our conversation. I appreciate your desire to expand your boundaries and boldly enter new markets.

- *Agreeable:* Thank you for our conversation. I appreciate your interest in improving communication and aligning thinking and ideas.

- *Conscientious:* Thank you for our conversation. I appreciate your commitment to establishing priorities and creating a smooth process to complete the project on time.

- *Emotionally stable:* Thank you for our conversation. I appreciate your objective insights driven by verifiable metrics.

EMAIL PART 2: CREATE ANXIETY BY ILLUSTRATING THE CONSEQUENCE OF DOING NOTHING

In Part 2, we present a brief portrait of life without taking action (or without using your solution), written to the person's Number 1 trait. The goal is to create just enough anxiety to make them feel uncomfortable. Recall that, as discussed in Chapter 18 on how to influence behavior, an understanding of benefits is not as powerful a motivator as the threat of loss. People are more likely to respond if you can tap into an unconscious fear that they might lose something if they fail to take action.

- *Open-minded:* Three years from now, imagine the situation with no real improvement.

- *Extroverted:* Without this initiative, think about another year of flat sales and the prospect of declining market share going forward.

- *Agreeable:* Consider that internal communication, collaboration, and morale could deteriorate because people feel that senior management is indifferent to their concerns.

- *Conscientious:* Think about the process continuing to be dysfunctional because the various business units aren't effectively communicating data.

- *Emotionally stable:* Consider the alternative—decisions based on pure speculation without metrics and facts to support them.

EMAIL PART 3: ISSUE THE CALL TO ACTION

Close your email by appealing again to the person's Number 1 trait:

- *Open-minded:* Let's move forward so that your innovative ideas will differentiate you from your competitors in the future.
- *Extroverted:* Let's move this initiative forward to expand market share.
- *Agreeable:* Let's partner and move our relationship forward.
- *Conscientious:* Let's work together to lay out the process, structure, and timeline now.
- *Emotionally stable:* Let's agree on the metrics of success so we can judge the initiative objectively.

EXAMPLE OF A THREE-PART EMAIL

Below is an example of an email I wrote to the chairman of a multibillion-dollar firm. He replied within 24 hours, inviting me to meet with him sometime in the following month. I considered his behavior, what he said in interviews that were easily found on the internet, and my personal introduction to him at an event. I ranked his Big Five personality traits as follows: agreeable, open-minded, extroverted, conscientious, and emotionally stable. With this background information in mind, I wrote the following email:

> Ed,
>
> Your recent interview about establishing a team-oriented attitude caught my attention. If your vision is to create a more collaborative culture, my counsel is to have the entire team understand their core personality strengths and how those strengths can be leveraged for optimal partner success. The research is profound, but simple. People are intrinsically motivated, contribute the most, and enhance the culture when they are leveraging their strengths.
>
> Firms that don't foster strategic collaboration with their clients will be viewed as just another commodity over the next 5 years.
>
> Let's meet to discuss implementing a program that will develop your partners into collaborative superstars. Please ask your admin to reach out to schedule a date.

This email begins with a statement that establishes resonance based on the recipient's top-ranked personality trait. A statement creating fear of loss or some level of anxiety relating to the consequence of nonaction follows. The final paragraph requests action using language that resonates with the recipient's top-ranked personality trait.

Consider using this template—it's a great tool, and it works!

PART **IV** STRATEGIC COACHING

STRATEGIC COACHING

Now we're going to expand on what you've learned about yourself and the building blocks of strategic leadership, to coach you to be a better coach.

You add the most strategic value in a role that aligns with your unique personality strengths. The distinction between adding strategic value and being a strategic leader is being able to drive business outcomes. Strategic leaders know both their own strategic value and how to capitalize on human talent to drive the economic transaction cycle to obtain superior results. They orchestrate human potential into dynamic transactional systems.

What ingredients go into orchestrating human potential into dynamic transactional systems to obtain superior results? How do you inspire high performance and get people aligned to make the sum of the whole greater than the individual parts?

We don't believe it's possible to become a strategic leader without being a skilled coach and mentor; having high self-awareness is essential. Thus far we've covered how to deeply understand your own personality and its strengths and shadows, how you add strategic value, and additional building blocks of strategic leadership.

People have different leadership styles that are strongly influenced by their dominant personality traits. But just as a conductor of one orchestra has a different style than another, all conductors strive for superior performance by focusing on certain essential elements. For leaders, this focus includes placing people in the right role based on their strengths, managing shadow behaviors and performance issues, encouraging efficiency, creating a winning and learning culture, and inspiring people toward a common vision.

What kind of leader are you, and what kind of leader do you aspire to be? Do you want to be someone who develops people, constantly challenging them to think critically? Do you want to create a culture of trust and authenticity where people grow, learn, and achieve exciting goals together? Do you want to give away your strengths and encourage your people to collaboratively do the same? Do you want your legacy to include being a coach and mentor—someone your people will remember fondly years from now?

21 YOUR LEADERSHIP STYLE

Consider the ranking of your own Big Five personality traits. We've already seen that your personality impacts how you communicate, process information, and respond to your environment. Let's explore how your highest and lowest ranked traits may affect your leadership and coaching style.

OPEN-MINDED

Highest Ranked Trait

Leaders whose Number 1 personality trait is open-minded enjoy planning and thinking about the future. Contemplating how events might unfold takes up a lot of mental energy, however. These leaders might procrastinate and put off activities they consider tedious or uninteresting. It can be difficult for them to stay focused. They have no time for repetitive and boring tasks. They enjoy creative and innovative activities, not grinding it out and crossing items off a list of daily objectives. They love developing ideas and brainstorming options.

https://doi.org/10.1037/0000391-022
Becoming a Strategic Leader: Capitalize on the Power of Your Personality, by G. W. Watts & L. Blazek

I'm an instant star. Just add water and stir.
–David Bowie, in *Valentines and Vitriol*

Lowest Ranked Trait

Leaders who rank open-minded as their Number 5 trait focus primarily on daily objectives, often failing to adequately plan for future events. They may have difficulty picturing how discrepant concepts have an underlying theme. Becoming more innovative and creative is a challenge. It's easy for them to throw cold water on ideas or get into a rut in the way they think and manage. To counterbalance these tendencies, they should attempt to branch out, seek input from open-minded creative types, and really listen to what they have to say. It's good practice for them to occasionally step out of their comfort zone by experiencing something new and completely different.

EXTROVERTED

Highest Ranked Trait

Extroverted leaders frequently come from business development. They act and behave much as they did when they had daily interface with clients and prospects. They often use their extroversion to sell their way out of situations. Being naturally exuberant, they desire a motivating, charged atmosphere. They're constantly on the move. Concentrating on details that should be managed isn't necessarily on their agenda. To compensate, an operational infrastructure, including a strong administrator, should be in place to handle the important and necessary details. The good news is that extroverted leaders are comfortable interacting with people and can contribute to a collaborative environment and making things happen in the field.

I'm the greatest thing that ever lived. I shook up the world!
–Muhammad Ali, Miami Beach Convention Center, 1964

Lowest Ranked Trait

Leaders who rank extroverted as their Number 5 trait don't want to be out shaking hands or attending business or social events, yet they know these activities play an important role in success. Such leaders tend to be internally focused and are likely to be strong with processes, organization, and follow through; it's here that they can help their people be more successful. They should attempt to engage and interface directly with colleagues and clients. Because interpersonal dynamics are real work, they should consider inviting extroverts to join them when attending business events to provide support in situations that involve network expansion.

AGREEABLE

Highest Ranked Trait

Agreeable leaders value social harmony. They are naturally empathetic, cooperative, and considerate. They believe in trust and collaboration. They strive for fairness through compromise. Because of their affable style, agreeable leaders may fail to take decisive action in moving disruptive personnel or nonproducers off the team. Sometimes leaders need to take a firm position, which isn't always easy for agreeable types. Agreeable leaders are natural peacekeepers; tough love, negotiation from strength, and managing conflict can be uncomfortable for them. They should be aware that they're prone to compromise too soon or to give in to aggressive, dominant individuals too quickly.

A genuine leader is not a searcher for consensus but a molder of consensus.
–Dr. Martin Luther King, Jr., National Labor Leadership Assembly for Peace, 1967

Lowest Ranked Trait

Leaders who rank agreeable as their Number 5 trait can be unpleasant, rude, and dismissive. They might overreact and create unnecessary stress. Their disagreeable nature may emanate from an unconscious need for attention. These leaders tend to discourage exploring alternatives and issues. As a result, innovation, open communication, and collaboration often aren't part of the culture. To counteract this tendency, they should plan well-thought-out agendas with appropriate structure when dealing with complex topics or problems. Practicing the "yes, and . . ." technique and committing to being more positive are difficult but worthy objectives.

CONSCIENTIOUS

Highest Ranked Trait

Conscientious leaders love to plan their work and work their plan. They set up excellent systems and processes; their office is run with efficiency. They set an example of how to be better organized for success. A challenge for the conscientious type is remaining too rooted in process to pay attention to the big picture. Being overly focused on solving operational or internal issues can leave little time for idea generation and strategic thinking. Initiating approach behavior, holding deep conversations, and displaying empathy aren't always high priorities for such leaders.

Genius is 1% inspiration and 99% perspiration.

−attributed to Thomas Edison

Lowest Ranked Trait

Leaders who rank conscientious as their Number 5 trait probably aren't well organized. Their office may be chaotic unless they hire an admin or business manager to ensure the place is well run. They have a strong tendency to wait until the last minute to take on a task or meet a deadline. They'd likely choose to be out with colleagues or clients rather than analyzing data or working on the latest internal report. They should delegate detail and processes so nothing falls through the cracks.

EMOTIONALLY STABLE

Highest Ranked Trait

Emotionally stable leaders run the office by the numbers with close scrutiny. They'll ensure that there is an objective basis for decision making and help people by encouraging them to be rational in their thinking. Such leaders won't necessarily provide the excitement and adrenaline the team might need. They may have difficulty connecting emotionally with others. Holding deep conversations and exhibiting empathy aren't likely to be among their strongest attributes. They should attempt to become more tuned in to the feelings and emotions of people around them.

For me, it is always important that I go through all the possible options for a decision.

−Angela Merkel, *Vanity Fair*, 2014

Lowest Ranked Trait

Leaders who rank emotionally stable as their Number 5 trait can be demonstrative and might wear their heart on their sleeve. This behavior can create a negative atmosphere, stifling teamwork and open communication. Unnecessary outbursts will ultimately erode respect. Most employees can't thrive in this type of work environment. They'll be less likely to take risks or to think creatively. These leaders need to pay attention to what events trigger specific, negative emotions and should take small steps toward getting themselves under control in the workplace.

Your Number 1 and Number 5 Traits

If you reflect on these descriptions, you can clearly see how your Number 1– and Number 5–ranked traits impact your behavior and leadership style. We've stated this before: No one trait is any better than another, and your Number 5 trait isn't necessarily a weakness. It's just your least natural orientation, so it's up to you to manage around it.

DON'T FORGET YOUR NUMBER 2 TRAIT

Your Number 1 personality trait reveals your natural personality strength, but keep in mind that your Number 2 trait impacts how your Number 1 trait manifests. Your Number 2 trait activates and channels your Number 1 trait.

For example, let's say my Number 1 trait is extroverted and my Number 2 trait is conscientious. This combination means that I enjoy people and that my leadership style reflects the fact that I like to engage and interact with others. I am also organized and will follow up to be sure administrative matters are managed, processes are in place, and deadlines are met.

What if my Number 1 trait is extroverted, but my Number 2 trait is open-minded? This fusion means that I enjoy engaging and interacting with others but also naturally think creatively. I like leading strategy sessions, whiteboarding ideas and visualizing future scenarios. An extroverted and conscientious leader is very different from an extroverted and open-minded leader.

Let's take another example. If my Number 1 trait is emotional stability and my Number 2 trait is agreeable, my leadership style is making rational and objective decisions while collaborating and partnering effectively, either internally or externally. The fusion will result in a measured, objective leadership style, coupled with a desire to positively affect culture through my decision making.

What if my Number 1 trait is emotional stability, but my Number 2 trait is extroverted? This combination means that I will still be driven by rational, quantitative metrics but that I also love presenting and engaging with people. This combination is quite powerful in that many emotionally stable types don't have the interpersonal skills to persuade others to buy into them and their ideas. An emotionally stable and agreeable leader is quite different from an emotionally stable and extroverted leader.

These examples demonstrate how the Number 2 trait directs the personality energy orientation. Think about your top two traits in combination and how they impact your leadership and coaching style. Your strategic value is driven by your dominant personality traits, and you will have the most success if you build your leadership responsibilities around your career brand and career branding statement.

BEING THE LEADER PEOPLE WANT TO FOLLOW

Top employees have choices. They can stay with you or respond to a recruiter's call. Having a merely cordial relationship with your people is increasingly not enough. Your relationship with employees is analogous to the relationship a business development professional has with clients. If either person doesn't add value as a trusted strategic partner and adviser, they'll be viewed as a commodity. Commodity or tactical managers are expendable and easily replaceable. Add value through activating your own personality strengths, giving away those strengths, and developing the strengths of individual team members.

Commodity or tactical managers are expendable and easily replaceable.

Most companies require leaders to complete formal performance evaluations of their direct reports. You may even be required to go through the process of force ranking your team. We'd like you to take a few minutes now and rank your people again. This time, really reflect on how much value they contribute to overall team success. How you define "value" is up to you.

Now, let's divide the list into thirds so you can clearly see who is above and below the mean. It's the leader's job to find a way to improve employees' performance from a C to a B and a B to an A and to continue to challenge and retain top performers.

So, what are you doing as a leader to motivate and create loyalty among your best people? How do you plan to raise the game of the average performer while managing the least effective performers? When was the last time you had a meaningful discussion with your direct reports about their personality strengths and how you can help them be more successful? If you aren't comfortable having this type of dialogue, keep reading. In Chapter 22, we provide you with a template for turning a discussion about performance into a positive coaching experience. If you don't actively take an interest in the career development of your people, you'll eventually lose their loyalty to your leadership.

GROW AS A LEADER

Think about a leader who inspired you to greater performance. What was it about that person and the culture they created that you respected and admired? How did that leader communicate? How did they motivate? Did they provide needed resources? Did they run political interference so you were better able to do your job? Did you want to do well, not just for yourself, but also for them and your team?

Now think about a leader who exhibited the opposite dynamic. Did they worry more about managing up than they did about managing and mentoring you? Did they have unrealistic expectations? Was their behavior driven solely by metrics? Did you believe they were out for themselves, regardless of how much they talked about being team oriented? Did they withhold information? Did they play favorites? Did they have poor listening skills? Did they treat people disrespectfully? Did they stifle an open and honest flow of information? Did they motivate by fear?

Do you do any of these things?

22 PERFORMANCE MANAGEMENT

This chapter is about helping your people capitalize on their individual personality strengths, manage around their weaknesses, and maximize their contribution to team success. We present a step-by-step approach to turning performance evaluation into a positive experience.

PERFORMANCE REVIEWS

Companies have long struggled with the issue of measuring performance and delivering employee evaluations. Regardless of whether it's called an "appraisal," an "evaluation," or a "review," the practice is fraught with deep flaws. The exercise creates resentment, damages morale, and contributes to a stressful work environment. Psychological studies show that the review process activates the fight-or-flight response, diminishes creativity, and heightens defensiveness. If you've ever had a negative or unfair evaluation, you surely understand this to be true.

https://doi.org/10.1037/0000391-023
Becoming a Strategic Leader: Capitalize on the Power of Your Personality, by G. W. Watts & L. Blazek

Yet, despite the negative consequences, most companies continue to engage in performance appraisals. Part of the reason is internal policy related to documenting poor performance. There's also the assumption that a review is an effective means of correcting or improving behavior; the idea is that people must be made aware if they're performing unsatisfactorily or if some aspect of their performance needs improvement.

There's no question that performance appraisals can negatively affect morale. Any low rating is often interpreted as personal and is emotionally damaging. The practice of forced ranking makes the entire process even worse, especially for high-functioning teams. Even top producers who are marked "does not meet expectations" on some aspect of their performance will talk about that rating years later.

There are alternatives to the uncomfortable ritual of sitting down with direct reports and discussing how they can improve. A number of progressive companies have actually ended the practice of performance appraisals altogether. But this also eliminates the opportunity for the positive professional development that results from holding deep discussions about performance. We advocate a new approach that solves this dilemma. Now is the time to embrace a more constructive and productive process.

Companies are increasingly acknowledging the importance of talent management. Firms don't need as many employees as they used to, but the ones they need are often expected to play a larger and more important role. When an employee isn't performing at the level you expect, there's a strong chance that either their core personality strengths aren't a good match for the role or they have a prevailing and immature shadow to their Number 1– or 2–ranked personality trait. Before you sit down with each person, have them rank order their Big Five personality traits and choose a positive and a shadow descriptor for their Number 1 and 2 traits.

COACHING TO PERSONALITY STRENGTHS

When discussing an employee's personality strengths, you'll want to focus on the top two traits. As you now know, when a person's top two traits are fused, the resultant energy is their preferred way of transacting in their business ecosystem. You'll want to understand each person's two strongest personality traits and how they reinforce each other. Encourage people to drill down by asking how they determined their Big Five ranking. What characteristics and behaviors associated with their top two traits do they most closely identify with? If they could exclusively do any one thing on their job, what would it be? What are they doing when they're in the zone and experiencing peak performance?

Understand each person's two strongest personality traits and how they reinforce each other.

Think about adjusting your language as you have these conversations. You already know that when you use language that resonates with a person's dominant personality trait, you'll have a much better chance of being heard and understood. And the more you and your direct report connect, working together to explore ways to capitalize on their strengths, the better everything will be.

How can you motivate and coach to each personality type? Here's what you can expect:

- *Open-minded:* Open-minded people are motivated when they visualize the future and imagine scenarios. You inspire open-minded people by coaching to their life 3 years out. Describe how you see the person's future if they commit to daily objectives, then help turn this 3-year vision into concrete reality. Give them challenging assignments that tap into their creativity and original resourcefulness. Open-minded types need to be reminded to keep their eye on the prize. Without focus, they can be scattered and live in the clouds too much.

- *Extroverted:* Extroverted people are energized when they're actively expanding their ecosystem. Introduce them to a new business partner or to influencers within your organization. Include them in meetings, and attend professional events together. Extroverted people will be motivated and energized in a position that involves interfacing and connecting with others. They enjoy extending their ego into their environment. A pure extrovert is a hunter by nature. But they often don't hunt strategically, and they may diffuse energy by being all over the map. Help them target their efforts to make the best use of their time and talent.

- *Agreeable:* Motivating agreeable people stems from the perception that you're supportive and a success partner. They value honest, egoless communication. Be genuine and straightforward. They want closeness, support, and the feeling of a trusted relationship. Agreeable types are motivated when forming internal and external partnerships. Assign them to projects or to a team where collaboration is paramount. Because of their amicable nature, they may need coaching to find a comfortable way to be more assertive when challenging people to meet deadlines and achieve goals.

- *Conscientious:* You'll motivate conscientious people by helping them structure a plan that connects with their strengths—one that has specific data points and requires organizational skills. Conscientious types want a well-thought-out, detailed path to success. Offer them a step-by-step plan with behavioral action items on daily, weekly, and monthly checklists. Conscientious people have strong work habits, but they can be rigid and need coaching on how to modify their response to altered circumstances or conditions.

- *Emotionally stable:* Motivation for emotionally stable people happens when metrics are agreed to and the terms of your relationship are spelled out and agreed upon. They're most comfortable when performance is measured against a well-articulated plan. They are optimistic when metrics are plausible and credible; they see themselves as competent and capable of accomplishing goals. They can, at times, be judgmental and condescending. People with high emotional stability are head driven and often don't show empathy or feelings because of their rationality and objectivity. You can coach them to work toward striking more of a head–heart balance.

CAREER BRAND COACHING EXERCISE

The two positive descriptors in a career brand are powerful. They provide insight into employees' personality strengths. This fusion of descriptors is their career brand, indicating where their positive energy comes from and how they add strategic value to your team. The more time they spend engaging in activities that align with that career brand, the more success they'll experience.

Have each employee choose two positive descriptors, one from their Number 1 trait and one from their Number 2 trait. Next, ask them to look up each descriptor and write down the salient and meaningful portions of each definition. From there, they should also consider what other descriptors from their top two traits feel and sound most relevant to them. Then ask them to connect those descriptors to the activities they're engaged in when they lose track of time and are in a zone state. How can they use their brand to achieve important goals in their present role?

People may experience a cognitive struggle when assigning language to their unique strengths to create a career branding statement. That's OK. The process of deep introspection is important. A branding statement that captures the essence of who you are is an anchor. It builds confidence. Share your branding statement, and get your people excited about being able to articulate who they are when they're at their best.

For example, let's say that a person's Number 1 trait is open-minded and their Number 2 trait is extroverted. They choose "inspirational" as the first descriptor and "performer" as the second descriptor. This person's career brand is "inspirational performer." A unique branding statement could be, "I inspire people to believe in themselves." Once they have created the statement, explain that it's going to become their personal brand—how they define themselves to their business ecosystem. Have them place the two descriptors and branding statement somewhere prominent to reflect upon every day.

Most of the time, when people are experiencing peak performance, their descriptors and branding statement are strongly connected to this activity. This exercise helps crystallize their thinking by using precise language to describe where they spike—their outlier personality strengths. This simple process enables each person to acknowledge how their career brand is being activated when they're performing at their best. This exercise is incredibly powerful, motivating, and potentially career and life changing.

COACHING TO WEAKNESSES

In performance discussions, it's important to explain that the Number 5–ranked personality trait is different from the shadow of their Number 1 and 2 traits. That is, the Number 5 trait is where they're least strong from a personality trait perspective—this trait is not their natural orientation. The shadow is the immature energy of their Number 1 and 2 traits.

A less threatening atmosphere is created when each person identifies their Number 5 trait and shadow descriptors, then relates how they may have affected performance. Let your people know that you're having similar conversations with everyone, and that you've done these exercises yourself. Because everyone, even you, has a Number 5 trait and shadow, there's a logical behavioral science basis for the discussion. Emphasizing this science basis depersonalizes the conversation and creates a more positive and productive exchange.

Because everyone, even you, has a Number 5 trait and shadow, there's a logical behavioral science basis for the discussion.

THE NUMBER 5 TRAIT

If a person is in a role aligning with their natural personality strengths, they should be activating their Number 1 and 2 traits. If the Number 5 trait is causing a performance problem, it's quite likely that the person is in the wrong role in that it doesn't align well with their natural abilities.

For example, let's assume that you work in a major insurance company and manage a person who's responsible for coordinating customer service for a large client. This person's top two traits are agreeable and conscientious. They build strong relationships, empathize, and collaborate while handling the details. They follow up and make certain nothing slips through the cracks. This role is aligned with the person's natural strengths. They're in the right role.

Let's assume this person's Number 5 trait is open-minded. As long as they meet a threshold of ability to see the big picture and anticipate where problems may arise in the future, the Number 5 trait isn't likely to be a factor in their success. You've essentially hired right if their Number 5 trait has little or no impact on their performance.

Here are some coaching tips for people with each Number 5 trait:

- *Open-minded:* People whose Number 5 trait is open-minded have challenges thinking theoretically and in the abstract. They tend not to be future oriented. They can get into a rut and become overly focused on tactics. They can also miss the forest for the trees because they tend to concentrate on what's in front of them at any particular moment. Involving them in more strategic discussions or group brainstorming sessions will help them see the big picture, giving them a greater appreciation for out-of-the-box thinking and the contribution of others.

- *Extroverted:* If a person's Number 5 trait is extroverted, they're more apt to leverage their technical expertise. These types gravitate toward positions where the ecosystem is permanent, where they aren't expected to have a lot of different and new interpersonal contact. Your coaching should urge them to occasionally get off the sidelines. Encourage them to expand their internal and external network by attending organizational events. Don't try to turn these people into extroverts. A worthy goal would be for them to become more confident and comfortable in their own skin and to feel at ease in outwardly facing situations.

- *Agreeable:* If agreeable is a person's Number 5 trait, expect a lot of ego and desire for control. These types can behave rudely and display little empathy. They are also prone to being narcissistic and self-absorbed and can quickly become irritated or annoyed. Coaching needs to center on encouraging them to look at situations from other people's perspectives. Help them understand the value of using reflective listening and the "yes, and . . ." technique. Emphasize the importance of team play and collaboration, and remind them that gaining a reputation of being disagreeable isn't going to serve them well in furthering their career.

- *Conscientious:* A person who ranks conscientious as their Number 5 trait will need coaching in managing detail, structure, process, and organization. They likely would rather seek out interpersonal interaction than handle paperwork and necessary administrative tasks. These types leave too much to chance, don't prepare well, and don't think out activities to construct a daily plan. Things can slip through the cracks because of their lack of organization. Encourage incremental steps to improve time and calendar management; many helpful suggestions are outlined in Chapter 24.

- *Emotionally stable:* For people whose Number 5 trait is emotionally stable, expect them to be emotional and not particularly interested in measurement or objectivity. They'll prefer to go by their instincts and plunge headlong into something, only to understand the ramifications later when details are overlooked or deadlines are missed. Try not to throw cold water on their creativity or lack of detail orientation. Periodically check in to ask questions around managing metrics or specific details. These types will not always think rationally and may be high-maintenance because of their emotionality.

COACHING TO THE SHADOW

Once your people have chosen shadow descriptors for their Number 1 and 2 traits, turn the discussion to identifying how these traits manifest and what, if any, impact they have on performance. As you know, all personality strengths have a shadow. If the positive aspects of their dominant traits are mature and their shadow characteristics are under control, there won't be an issue. If the shadow dominates, however, or infects behavior to the extent that it hurts the person's overall value to the team, then there's coaching to be done.

Shadow examples include the following:

- the open-minded person who lacks focus and fails to meet deadlines
- the extroverted person with poor listening skills who dominates conversations

- the agreeable person who has low self-esteem and worries too much about what others think
- the conscientious person whose rigidity is interfering with open communication and teamwork
- the emotionally stable person whose tendency to judge makes them difficult to work with

The benefit of having people identify their specific shadow characteristics is the opportunity to have an open discussion about what action, if any, they need to take to manage their behavior. Again, this discussion will have a positive and productive tone because they, not you, choose their shadow descriptors.

BENEFITS OF OUR APPROACH TO COACHING

Most people don't understand their natural personality strengths or have the confidence to know how to capitalize on them. Because a person's weaknesses are not typically discussed in a positive and supportive context, they can feel threatened and uncomfortable talking about their weaknesses. This may be the first time your people have been coached in how to capitalize on personality strengths and manage shadow behavior.

This may be the first time your people have been coached in how to capitalize on personality strengths and manage shadow behavior.

In your conversations, be sure to explore the following:

- How did you determine your Number 1 and 2 traits? How do you think the two positive descriptors, when fused, represent your career brand?

- Share ways you believe you can use your career brand more effectively in your role.

- Let's discuss your Number 5 trait and the tasks in your job description that align with that trait. Can those tasks be delegated to someone else or managed differently?

- Let's discuss the shadow descriptors you've selected. How do they impact your job performance, productivity, and satisfaction?

- What action steps can you take to negate the effects of your shadow, and how can I help you?

This process will help you obtain a better understanding of your team. You'll gain insight into who's in the right job and who's not, who you should reposition to enable them to contribute in a way that optimizes their personality strengths, and who, with just a little bit of coaching, can overcome any negative effects of their Number 5 trait and shadow. Strategic leaders orchestrate human potential into dynamic transactional systems. Align personality strengths to job requirements. Putting the right people in the right role is the best organizational development strategy there is.

Align personality strengths to job requirements.

Through this process, you may also learn something about your own leadership style. You could discover that your dominant personality traits are the same as the people you most resonate with. You may also find that people who are less like you are those you rely on to accomplish tasks you either don't do well or have no interest in doing. Because those tasks are most likely associated with your Number 5 trait, they will require the most concentrated effort from you. As you have conversations, you may also become aware of why you connect or don't connect with someone, and how the language you use may or may not be resonating and why.

Finally, you may gain insight into when and why conflict among team members occurs. Remember that people with similar personalities tend to naturally resonate with each other. We like people who are like ourselves. When there is tension or conflict, you should be better positioned to manage the situation: You now understand that the root cause may be differing perceptions and priorities that are personality driven. This knowledge is freeing because it's more objective. It eliminates personal judgment and replaces it with a behavioral science approach to solving negative interpersonal dynamics.

FOLLOW UP

We encourage you to ask each of your people to write a summary of your discussion that includes action steps you both have agreed to. Yes, this process takes energy, time, and commitment. It's ultimately your decision as to whether you believe the benefits are worth the effort. We strongly believe they are.

23 CREATING A WINNING CULTURE

Strategic leaders cultivate positive psychological dynamics that drive and direct values and behavior. In this chapter, we discuss five ways to positively influence culture: optimism, collectivity, learning, selflessness, and imitative behavior. We encourage you to reflect on your own style and identify where you might focus additional effort and energy.

OPTIMISM

We understand that business professionals leave companies to further their careers. More and more people perceive themselves as free agents, and loyalty isn't as important as opportunity. But joining an environment where people are improving, growing, and succeeding provides optimism to all, especially new hires.

We have defined a strategic leader as someone who orchestrates human potential into dynamic transactional systems. Instilling a culture of optimism and confidence is at the core of what motivates and inspires performance. If

https://doi.org/10.1037/0000391-024
Becoming a Strategic Leader: Capitalize on the Power of Your Personality, by G. W. Watts & L. Blazek

people work hard and do what's expected, they can, and will, be successful. It's invaluable when people are optimistic and believe in the leader, and the leader returns the belief. There's nothing that builds confidence and optimism quite like someone whom you respect believing in you. From a psychoanalytical perspective, senior leaders are like wonderful parents who say with conviction to their child, "We believe in your ability to be successful." When a child convincingly hears this from their parents, it cements a deep well of confidence. Obviously, a leader is not a parent, but their seniority places them in a position to be highly impactful on individual achievement and team dynamics.

People naturally want to do a quality job. Creating and reinforcing an optimistic environment brings out the best in people. Employees should know that if they don't meet the responsibilities of the position, they'll eventually be asked to move on. But losing employees is costly and disruptive, and having unhappy or unproductive people on your team negatively impacts everyone.

Each personality type will pursue a different workplace experience and will naturally excel in different phases of the strategic transacting model. The open-minded person will enjoy a position that requires creativity, imagination, and contemplation of future events. The extroverted person will love to present and connect with others; attending functions and representing the team outside the work environment energize them. The agreeable person will want to work collaboratively and partner; they have high emotional intelligence and like being on a team. The conscientious person will love organizing, establishing processes, and managing projects or details. The emotionally stable person will enjoy assessing metrics against criteria, evaluating data, and making decisions that are rationally driven.

Beyond question, people are happiest and intrinsically motivated when using and expanding upon their strengths. In essence, they're self-managed from a motivational perspective.

People are happiest and intrinsically motivated when using and expanding upon their strengths.

The most admired companies strive for more than just quality job performance. They want employees to be optimistic, happy, and even passionate about their work. Job satisfaction is enhanced when roles align with core personality strengths. When this alignment occurs, work isn't just work; it's meaningful and personally rewarding. Motivation then becomes intrinsic.

When a job offer is made, it's always made in good faith. Everyone wants to do well, but from a statistical perspective, come performance appraisal time, most people are eventually placed into the "average performer" or "meets expectations" category. Performance can improve when strong leaders passionately support and believe in their people. As a team, by definition, members are allies in the quest for achievement. It cultivates optimism when the team sets attainable (but stretch) goals, is surrounded by positive energy and high-performing colleagues, and has a leader who believes in them. This isn't naivete or an unrealistic understanding of the daily business challenges. It's the subtle difference that makes people feel good about their work environment.

Foster an atmosphere of realistic confidence with optimism as its foundation. This is an important yet largely unrecognized component of strategic leadership.

COLLECTIVITY

The team, as an aggregate, is greater than the sum of its members. Being on a team of people who are all experiencing the same pressures, deadlines, unappreciative clients, meeting and presentation preparation, stressful travel, and disappointments means that you're not alone. This realization is often referred to as *universality,* or the awareness that your concerns or problems are not unique or rare.

Being part of a well-functioning team provides psychological safety. Each team member feels they belong. They value the team and feel valued by the team. There is a collective consciousness of self-esteem. Most people understand norms of behavior and thus try their best to be good team players. There is a collective goodwill. Yes, there's internal competition, but there's also group support.

In a well-functioning team culture, self-disclosure is an important contribution to collectivity. The deeper the self-disclosure, the more the team will bond because they understand they have a lot in common. One purpose of periodic meetings is to create a sense of collectivity by promoting meaningful and consequential self-disclosure.

One purpose of periodic meetings is to create a sense of collectivity by promoting meaningful and consequential self-disclosure.

Typical disclosures include the unrealistic expectations of a challenging client and exasperation from managing internal partners or processes. Encouraging open communication and disclosure gives the leader the opportunity to publicly acknowledge issues and lead a discussion that delivers insights. When people understand that everyone shares similar disappointments and frustrations, a feeling of normalcy or universality is enhanced.

Coaching Collectivity

Ultimately, with effective coaching, the team will unite behind a common mission or goal. Even if team members are in different geographic locations, the bond linking them to one another and to the team as a whole will strengthen. Strong teams resemble a family, and the family feeling provides a sense of cohesiveness and collectivity.

People who feel safe can more easily express emotions and feelings. In psychoanalytic psychology, this release of emotions is referred to as "catharsis," stemming from the Greek word meaning "purification" or "cleansing." If there's a strong level of collectivity, people can, and should, experience occasional intense emotional releases in a tolerant and supportive atmosphere. After the release, it's back to work, but now with a sense of camaraderie. Teams need a certain swagger—not egotistical, but confident, based on realistic optimism. Facilitating cathartic expression can have a powerful positive impact on group dynamics. People with some personality traits, particularly extroverts, need it more than others.

How does each personality trait contribute to team energy and collectivity? The following are examples of how these traits add strategic value to the team and to you as leader:

- *Open-minded:* Open-minded people contribute by asking theoretical questions and thinking conceptually about future states. They're often creative and good at leading brainstorming sessions.

- *Extroverted:* Extroverted people like to present, so they enjoy being up-front, getting attention, and putting on a show. They lend enthusiasm and contribute to an upbeat spirit. They like to get out into their environment and make things happen. They set the pace in meeting new people and pursuing opportunities.

- *Agreeable:* Agreeable people are peacemakers. They diffuse conflict and smooth ruffled feathers. They're strong team players, even if they aren't demonstrative. They exhibit a calm presence, harmonize, and get people on the same page.

- *Conscientious:* Conscientious people focus on detail, implementation, and process. They're highly organized and see that tasks are completed. They create lists and design steps to accomplish goals. They can help run the team operationally.

- *Emotionally stable:* Emotionally stable people generally have a solid and objective point of view based on facts and metrics. They put the brakes on ideas that sound better than they really are. They act deliberately and don't let feelings and emotions skew their responses to situations. Emotionally stable types can contribute by providing alternative points of view based on rational and objective thinking.

Fostering Collectivity

Your team members have different strengths based on their personality trait ranking. Take advantage of this by helping the entire team learn how each top trait manifests in successful behavior. Ask top performers with differing Number 1 traits to discuss how that trait helps them be successful, as follows:

- *Open-minded:* If you have a top performer who's open-minded, ask them to share how they connect the dots to form a unique strategic solution, either internally or externally. These types are creative and inquisitive. Have them share examples of how they used their creativity or when brainstorming ideas created a positive outcome.

- *Extroverted:* If you have a top performer who's extroverted, ask them to share their strategies for getting past barriers or expanding their network. What do they do to effectively grow internal or external relationships? Can they provide an example of how to be aggressive in approaching a business situation or opportunity?

- *Agreeable:* If you have a top performer who's agreeable, ask what their strategy is in listening effectively and how they think about partnering relationships. Have them share examples of when they successfully managed a challenging political situation or of how they approach conflict resolution.

- *Conscientious:* If you have a top performer who's conscientious, ask how they break down work into manageable steps. How do they develop processes and ensure quality execution? How do they stay organized? Can they give an example of how their detail orientation contributed to solving a problem?

- *Emotionally stable:* If you have a top performer who's emotionally stable, ask tough but fair questions based upon facts. How do they stay focused and prioritize time? What metrics do they hold themselves to? How did they successfully approach a problem using objectivity and rationality?

The purpose of asking questions of top performers with different Number 1 traits is to foster an atmosphere of collectivity. After facilitating this discussion, think about how your team responded. What was the body language and level of enthusiasm in the room? Do you sense that this was a growth experience and that team members gained insight into the successful behavior of others?

In our experience, when people gain an understanding of how each person's strengths contribute to the success of the team, a new level of maturity, respect, and appreciation emerges among team members. Remember, you need everyone pulling in the same direction to drive the economic transaction cycle to obtain superior results.

LEARNING

Learning can often take a back seat to other priorities, but it's an important contributor to positive team dynamics. There are three key types of learning: knowledge expansion, accurate thinking, and affective learning.

Knowledge Expansion

People want to feel that they're in the know. Nothing's worse for morale than hearing through the grapevine about significant organizational changes or, even worse, bad news from "corporate." Early distribution of information and clarification of known specifics are essential to minimizing stress and uncertainty. You can create a culture that supports an industry-smart team by sharing pertinent and important information, what's happening within the industry, any looming internal management or procedural changes, and anything else of significance that might impact the group.

It's always a good idea to be on the lookout for tips, information, or ideas that expand knowledge and support success. Think of your team as a learning organization where people are striving to improve and grow professionally. Be on the lookout for any articles that may be of interest. Encourage team members to do the same for each other. When you offer the gift of knowledge, there's an understood bond that sends the message that you're all in this together. Professionals always appreciate thoughtful efforts to help them learn and grow. Expanding their knowledge is at the heart of building loyalty, cohesiveness, and a learning organization.

Accurate Thinking

As part of promoting learning, leaders provide alternatives and suggestions on how to achieve goals, but people are too often overly hopeful and unrealistic. They should feel hope, but hope based on accurate thinking. Accurate thinking is objective and rational. As we've discussed, people who are head driven are more naturally prone to rationality. Heart-driven types will more naturally act on feelings and emotions rather than facts.

Both head- and heart-driven personality types can fall prey to inaccurate thinking. Thinking accurately sometimes means taking a risk and defying your own natural instincts. People can increase the accuracy of their thinking by seeking outside input. In other words, they need to be confident enough to challenge themselves. Challenging oneself not only is healthy but shows real maturity. Create an atmosphere where people feel safe to question their own thinking or the status quo.

Observe your people's behavior, and constructively comment on ineffective thought patterns or actions that don't facilitate goal attainment. Each of the Big Five personality traits can manifest in behaviors that reflect inaccurate thinking. Open-minded people can dream too much and lack focus, extroverts can spin their wheels and overcommit, agreeable people can waste time on people who won't further their goals, conscientious people can spend too much time on minutiae and data analysis, and emotionally stable people can be judgmental and negative.

Accurate thinking is particularly necessary when you are managing new hires and less experienced employees. Have a dependable model for each position you manage. You should be clear on exactly what personality traits are required for success in a specific role. Ensure that your employees are thinking accurately about what's expected and how their performance will be measured.

Affective Learning

Affective learning involves attitudes, motivation, and values. Ideally, employees should describe themselves as happy, goal-striving professionals who value long-term reciprocal relationships. Hopefully, they have a strong level of desire to continue to learn and grow into the next opportunity. As a leader, you should be interested in helping your people further develop their careers.

Affective learning is learning through interacting and receiving feedback. Through your actions, people experience your leadership style and values. You know that each member of your team has a certain personality, and that you have a certain personality. Interaction between the personalities manifests energy. Now that you have a more complete understanding of your personality strengths, you can generate more productive and positive energy with everyone, not just with people who are like you.

Robust communication is the foundation of great on-the-job training. Imagine creating a team culture that includes ongoing training and professional growth and development. You would essentially be creating a learning organization that costs little relative to the rewards.

Employees gain a greater understanding of themselves when provided with insights and feedback. Through social modeling, strong team members provide examples of desirable skills and habits. Team meetings are a great place to practice and share new behaviors, to brainstorm, and to experiment with ideas without fear. Think of your team meetings as learning events, with you and your team creating each lesson plan.

SELFLESSNESS

An atmosphere of selflessness will improve collaboration and team dynamics. The more a leader is perceived as selfless, the better. We understand that most companies are organized like a wedding cake, with fewer positions at the top. But you can still be generous with perks, bonuses, special assignments, and recognition. A good example of this type of generosity is when a sales manager gives away a promising lead and forgoes personal gain. This type of selfless act makes an important statement to your people.

The more a leader is perceived as selfless, the better.

Lead your people—don't compete with them. We acknowledge and appreciate that sometimes working managers carry a bag, too; you also have individual productivity goals. But splitting the credit or commission whenever possible says quite a lot. It goes a long way toward contributing to a positive environment.

When leaders turn over a promising opportunity, they are demonstrating the renunciation of self. They give up something that would have provided a short-term benefit to pursue something with a potential long-term benefit, always based on a value system of wanting to help others succeed. When you demonstrate selflessness, you break down barriers and allow people to expand their thinking. It means you can be more genuine and authentic. When you don't act for personal gain and take the greater good into account, it shows you have confidence that the pie is ever expanding.

Fear of there not being enough money or opportunity for everyone shouldn't be a part of your belief system. When you believe there's enough for everyone, you inspire confidence and conviction. In such an optimistic environment, employees will feel a sense of safety. They'll begin to socially model these psychological dimensions of selflessness, creating a positive atmosphere and a framework for a socially effective team.

IMITATIVE BEHAVIOR

The predisposition to imitate is an innate human characteristic. It's common for people to want to imitate the behavior of others, especially those they hold in high esteem. We discussed the concept of social proof and herd behavior in Chapter 18. People want to act correctly, and they look to the behavior of others for cues.

Creating an atmosphere of frequent exchange through team sharing and mentoring from successful team members is a leadership challenge. Sharing in each other's professional growth should be encouraged; it creates a positive team dynamic. Especially for less experienced employees, imitating others' behavior or style is an important way to learn who they are and who they are not. Examining and studying the success of others, particularly in sales, is a useful learning pursuit. Some activities and behaviors will feel natural and some won't, depending on their dominant personality traits.

We know that people are going to be most successful when using their natural personality strengths, strengths that are individual to them. So, although imitative behavior is a common practice, it's important to coach your people that imitation is no substitute for understanding their own strengths and how they add strategic value.

ANALYZING PERSONAL EXPERIENCES

The following three examples show how a leader's personality drove culture and strategy. All three are related to C-suite positions I held at some point in my career.

John, the first CEO I reported to, was emotionally stable and conscientious. His strength was his evenness of temperament. He was a former fighter pilot, which was an excellent fit for a person with high emotional stability. It's just not a good idea for an emotionally unstable person to fly planes carrying nuclear weapons!

This organization had a sales-driven culture, and John's leadership was essential to its success. What I loved about John was his calm and rational nature. The company was run with a sense of fairness and integrity. Conflict was handled by carefully listening first, which was very important for the culture. Because it was a large sales organization, extroverts dominated the field. Being an emotionally stable person, he respected the salespeople, yet he looked at life dispassionately and metrically. He could defuse commission arguments with reasoned facts, in such a way that both sides could attest to his fairness. And he understood the value of training. He wanted an industry-smart team who were cognitive leaders of the profession. There was a real sense of collectivity and camaraderie; people liked and respected each other. There was competition, but it was always fair and positive.

The company was eventually sold, and John retired. Working for John taught me the importance of instilling optimism, fostering collectivity, and creating a learning environment that values selflessness. I also experienced firsthand how a leader's dominant personality traits direct corporate culture and strategy.

Andy, another CEO I worked for, was extroverted and open-minded. We worked for an operationally driven firm. As an extrovert, Andy was the captain; the team behaved like pirates. When he was brought in as CEO, he introduced a certain swagger to what had previously been a staid company. Andy was a great guy and a lot of fun. As a result of his extroverted leadership style, people became more confident and assertive. The atmosphere was exhilarating; there was a sense of collectivity and unison. People socialized outside work because they honestly enjoyed each other's company. And you would routinely find Andy and his extroverted personality at the center of it all.

As sometimes happens in business, board members got sideways with each other, Andy left, and the management team turned over. It was fun while it lasted, and once again, I experienced how a leader's dominant personality trait greatly influenced an organization's culture.

A third CEO I reported to was extroverted and emotionally stable. This was another operationally driven company. Mark was a charismatic, marketing-oriented leader who understood branding and telling a compelling story. Initially, when he joined the company, there was a sense of optimism, as the senior team believed in his vision. But second-round funding never materialized, and the company was put up for sale. The working environment became highly stressful, and a greedy everyone-for-themselves mentality began to take over.

It was with Mark that I experienced the shadow of extroversion and emotional stability all too well. In a relatively short period, Mark, a previously charismatic and deliberative (positive descriptors) leader, became a frenzied and calculating (shadow descriptors) leader. This example shows how a stressful situation can activate and energize shadow behavior. Mark, an immature leader, moved from the light to the shadow, transforming a positive and upbeat culture into a daily nightmare.

CULTURE MATTERS

To successfully create a sustainable, winning culture, the right dynamics need to align. Macro issues, such as not obtaining second-round funding, or a shift in business focus or strategy can derail even the most promising situations. The important takeaway is that in most circumstances, you really do have the power to create a positive winning culture. You can encourage an environment that fosters optimism, collectivity, learning, selflessness, and imitative behavior. You can have a profound and lasting impact on people's careers and their lives.

24 COACHING PRODUCTIVE WORK HABITS

Top performers have developed disciplined habits and practices that support their success. They understand that time is their greatest resource. They actively manage their calendar, emails, and paperwork. They do their homework, follow up, and follow through. Their activities always support their highest priority goals.

Having productive and efficient work habits can more quickly drive the transaction cycle. But not everyone is disciplined in how they manage their day. People become complacent and believe that for the most part, what they're doing is good enough. Head-driven personality types are naturally going to be organized, process driven, and discerning regarding how their time is spent. It's the heart-driven personality types who likely have the most work to do. But they can improve, despite the myriad of forces that make permanently adopting new behaviors a challenge.

Even if you aren't highly conscientious or emotionally stable, you can help instill certain habits and practices in your people that will lead to a more productive workforce. Even small changes in behavior can result in a

https://doi.org/10.1037/0000391-025
Becoming a Strategic Leader: Capitalize on the Power of Your Personality, by G. W. Watts & L. Blazek

more efficient work environment. Imagine if by being better organized, each person could gain an additional hour per week of high-value productivity.

JOB ANALYSIS

A job analysis may or may not apply in a particular situation. However, if it does, we encourage you to share an exercise with your people. First, ask them to take time and reflect on how they plan their week and work activities. How often do they think about how they allocate their time? Do they move from task to task and meeting to meeting feeling that there aren't enough hours in the day? Do daily activities support near-term goals and career goals?

Most people have items in their calendar or customer relationship management (CRM) software like "finish XYZ report" or "schedule a meeting with XYZ." These are tasks that don't involve planning or broader thinking. There isn't a road map to keep people on track to accomplish goals or prevent them from engaging in activities that don't support success.

The first step in prioritizing tasks and setting goals is to understand how time is spent. The process involves reviewing calendars, thinking about a typical work week or month, and estimating how much time is spent on various activities. Each person should create their own list of activities, noting the percentage of time they spend on each so that the total equals 100%.

The second step is for each person to create a task identification and prioritization template. Items could include routine job responsibilities, longer term projects or assignments, and tasks they take on or are assigned. Examples are "generate three new proposals," "schedule internal meetings on XYZ project," "arrange two prospect meetings," or "contact a current client to discuss project progress."

After listing these tasks, each person needs to categorize them by time frame: either less than or more than 30 days. Next, they should prioritize the list, or at least highlight the highest priority items. Separately, they should identify career goals that are more than a year out. All of the activities they undertake should be supportive of their longer term career goals.

Now ask your people to compare the items they identified as highest priority on the task list to the percentage of time they spend on each. It's often an "Aha!" moment when they see, in writing, how much time is spent on lower priority items and activities. Many people spend an inordinate amount of time on tasks and activities that are unrelated to their primary objectives. They get bogged down in the daily onslaught of emails, phone calls, and other distractions. Someone who is extroverted and agreeable can easily fall into the trap of spending too much time developing interpersonal relationships. The agreeable person can also have trouble saying no and will take on work that doesn't further their goals or that could be delegated to someone else.

Many people spend an inordinate amount of time on tasks and activities that are unrelated to their primary objectives.

The objective of this exercise is to create awareness in your people and confront them with how they're spending their time. It's also designed to guide them in creating a simple system of thinking less tactically by aligning activities with high-priority goals.

Now that your people have identified and prioritized tasks and goals, the last step is to create action items that will support those goals. Action items are created from the task list. For example, "complete client presentation" would become a specific actionable item with time carved out to stay on track. The action items are moved directly onto the calendar or CRM software.

The important result of this exercise is that the actionable items align with high-priority tasks, and people commit to acting on those items. Managing time this way will help people be more disciplined in their thinking. Your people should review and modify the task list and action items as priorities change and new opportunities arise.

This system is most effective when each person sets a goal to complete a certain number of action items per week. When they complete an item, they should replace it with another one. Once your people implement this process, you'll quickly begin to see results. There's a collectivism that begins to occur when everyone commits to checking off a specific number of action items per week. People remain focused on accomplishing high-priority tasks that support long-term goals. It's a highly motivating activity that contributes to positive team dynamics.

Even if this system has limited applicability within your specific business, consider the benefits of having people articulate exactly how they're spending their time and how those activities support success. The idea is to begin thinking less tactically about how work is accomplished.

Dominant personality traits impact everything we do. Characteristics of each of the Big Five traits may affect time management skills in the following ways:

- Open-minded people may be more focused on future objectives and less focused on those that need to be dealt with near term.

- Extroverted people are more likely to talk about getting something done than to follow through.

- Agreeable people are prone to spending too much time on other people's priorities at the expense of their own objectives.

- Conscientious people are organized and process driven, but they can over-think what needs to be done, waste time unnecessarily on minutiae, and not see the big picture.

- Emotionally stable people would be expected to have the strongest time management skills of any of the Big Five traits. Their deliberative, logical, and systematic nature should be an asset in prioritizing time and tasks.

DECLINING INVITATIONS

Highly successful people routinely decline invitations. They value time as a scarce resource that cannot be wasted. Do any of your people fall into the trap of accepting invitations even though they know they should be spending time on more productive activities? Do you?

Encourage people to think accurately when receiving an invitation or request. If it's not aligned with their highest priorities, they should decline it. It's good practice to decline at least one invitation per week. This can be very challenging for agreeable people, who have a tendency to say yes to almost everything. It might be something as simple as passing on an invitation for coffee or lunch. The idea is to spend the time freed up by declining the invitation on a high-priority activity.

In your group meetings, ask someone to give an example of when they declined an invitation and felt bad about it. Discuss whether their dominant personality trait might have been a factor in how they felt. Were there any repercussions to declining the invitation? Encourage people to look at whether they're really thinking accurately. It's empowering to quickly go through a mental assessment of whether an invitation will support stated priorities. The point is to focus on success. When that happens, the practice of selectively declining invitations should become routine.

EFFICIENCY

As you read this section, think about yourself and how you can coach your people. You may even pick up some helpful tips that will save you time and improve team productivity.

If you have stacks of paper on your desk or in your office that need to be acted on, do one of these things with every paper item:

- Handle every correspondence only once—act on it, scan and file it, or shred it.

- Consider carving out a window of time every day until your workspace is clear of paper.

If your email inbox is cluttered with messages that give you a daily reminder of how far behind you are, do one of these things with every email:

- Handle every correspondence only once—act on it, file it, or delete it.

- Create folders that correspond to the emails received and use them to file items for review at a future date. Work toward getting your inbox down to 25 messages or less.

- Consider challenging your team to better manage paper and emails. The people who do will feel lighter and more in control.

EMAIL USE

An email time saver is to schedule specific blocks of time in your calendar solely for the review of email messages. Resist the temptation to check messages more frequently.

We've just discussed the importance of efficiency, and there's no doubt that email is an efficient way of communicating. That said, we challenge you to view the world of electronic communications differently; leading by example can make a big difference. Ask yourself and your team four questions:

1. Think about the last time you scheduled an appointment by phone. When you did, was there an opportunity to create or deepen a relationship with an executive assistant or gatekeeper?

2. When was the last time you answered a question by picking up the phone instead of sending an email message? Could a simple phone call create an opportunity to ask one additional question that may give you information no one else has?

3. How many times have you had to send clarifying email messages because the recipient misunderstood or misinterpreted your first message? Email messages are very easy to misunderstand. If the back-and-forth process

clarifying what you meant is annoying and time consuming to you, how annoying do you think it is to the other person?

4. Have you ever sent an email thanking someone for a meeting? Wouldn't a phone call or handwritten thank you note be more personal? How do you feel when someone calls you or takes the time to send you a hand-written note?

We're always short on time, but when we use electronic communication, we often shortchange ourselves. Can we agree that conversations help build relationships, provide an opportunity to gain additional information, and reduce the probability of miscommunication? If this is true, then why do we use email so much?

We have two suggestions. First, instead of sending an email, pick up the phone or send a handwritten note. Force yourself to make five or even 10 phone calls per week instead of using email. Schedule those calls into your calendar. Second, when using email, always carefully reread every message you write so you're certain the grammar and spelling are correct. It's shocking how many messages have simple grammatical errors that spell check does not catch. Remember Malcom Gladwell's *Blink* and the concept of thin slicing: This rapid, unconscious mental processing influences how someone perceives you. Poorly worded or misspelled electronic communications can form a lasting negative impression.

SCHEDULING AND TIME MANAGEMENT

It's important to reinforce to your team that time is their most valuable asset. Every activity should be measured against the potential cost of the time it will take. We all know what high-cost transactions are: unnecessary meetings, long travel times that eat up chunks of your day, activities that don't support your personal and professional goals, and too much time socializing with clients or colleagues simply because you like them.

Every activity should be measured against the potential cost of the time it will take.

The calendar should be used to accomplish goals and ensure you're working on the things that are most important now. Your calendar reflects some of the most important decisions you make each day. Pay attention to the items you add to the calendar and how much time you allot for each.

Some people subscribe to the idea of categorizing activities as important or urgent. This strategy can be effective, but we encourage you to manage activities on the basis of their priority. To do this, you need to apply filters to those items that are most demanding of your time. Decide what items get some portion of your time, a reduced portion of your time, or no time at all.

Successful people actively manage their time and calendar, but this doesn't mean they take shortcuts. It means being smart, saying no when appropriate, and having a heightened awareness of the value of time. Most people don't have someone to manage their calendar, so it's really up to each individual. Not surprisingly, the Big Five personality traits are a factor here; for example, people with the conscientious personality trait are naturally more organized and disciplined when it comes to managing their time.

Calendar Management Survey and Tips

We suggest that you share the following survey and tips with your team. Facilitating a group discussion relating to calendar management is a good way to foster collectivity.

Which of the following items apply to you?

- You find you are constantly in back-to-back meetings.
- You feel your time is double-booked too often.
- You feel a lack of control over your day.
- You use more than one calendar and they're not synced.
- You initiate a meeting without a clear agenda or necessary preparation.
- You feel constantly rushed and often arrive late to meetings.
- You have a first come, first served mentality regarding scheduling.
- You occasionally miss a meeting because you forgot to enter it into your calendar.
- You don't use your calendar for all things important, including personal activities.
- You suddenly realize during the day or in the middle of the night that you aren't sure you entered something into your calendar.

The following calendar management tips can help you improve your time management:

- Every important item, whether business or personal, goes into your calendar.
- If your software allows, assign a color to each general category of activities, such as client meetings and internal meetings.
- Use only one calendar, or sync multiple calendars, so nothing slips through the cracks.

- Review whether items on your calendar are necessary and whether the amount of time allocated is appropriate.

- At the end of each day, review your calendar for accuracy. Once you've visualized your schedule for the next day, you can forget about it for the evening.

- Block out time in your calendar every day to use for thinking rather than reacting.

- To avoid distraction and save time, schedule a specific time in your calendar to review emails and voice mails.

- Leave gaps in your schedule so you have the flexibility to address new problems or opportunities that arise during the day.

- Well in advance, add easily foreseen or routine meetings to your calendar. If you know that a follow-up to a meeting is warranted, schedule the follow-up at the end of the meeting so you don't have to waste time doing it later.

- Avoid sending the message "When can we meet?" Unless you propose a specific date and time, this type of email is a time waster.

- Preempt urgent requests you know are coming by initiating a meeting to address them that fits your schedule.

- Next to the scheduled meeting or call, indicate in your calendar the purpose and your personal goals so you are focused and prepared.

Identifying areas of potential improvement through the survey and incorporating our calendar management tips will help your people develop better time management skills. Use of these tips also frees up the brain, allowing it to focus on higher level activities that support success.

MEETING PLANNING

Meeting planning might be one of the most overlooked processes in all of business. Every day, people at all levels go into internal and external meetings unprepared. We hear lots of excuses, but the common theme is that there are so many demands on people's time that they simply have to wing it and shortcut the planning process.

In advance of any meeting, it's good practice to formulate an agenda with thoughtful, open-ended questions. Remember our comments in Chapter 23 about value-added leaders: Everyone's time is valuable. Make your meetings meaningful by taking the time to develop a strategy that will enable you to deepen every discussion.

SET THE EXAMPLE

This chapter doesn't contain very exciting material, although some of you conscientious and emotionally stable types may disagree. We believe, however, that setting an example of best practices and providing coaching on habits and practices is important. Leadership is often about getting the little things right. Increased awareness among your people of maximizing how time is spent, improving organizational skills, and placing more focus on thinking about daily activities can make a noticeable improvement in team productivity.

25 TEAM BUILDING

One of the greatest franchises in the history of modern sports was the six-time National Basketball Association champion Chicago Bulls. Michael Jordan, their star player, is considered the finest athlete to ever play the game. When he was recruited to play for the Bulls in 1984, the franchise had one of the worst records in the NBA. Over the next few years, the team's record slowly began to improve. But anyone who watched them play could easily observe that having a superstar on the team was not enough to create a winning franchise. There was no team chemistry; something was clearly missing.

The turnaround began when the great coach Phil Jackson took the helm in 1989. He immediately understood that team members, Jordan in particular, were focused on individual achievement and not the success of the team. Jackson knew he had a challenge ahead of him. He would have to convince Jordan that he could have both the best individual statistics in the history of basketball and many team championships. He needed to persuade a superstar to subordinate his ego—to move from the shadow to the light.

Michael Jordan's Number 1 trait is emotional stability. We suspect that the positive descriptor for his Number 1 trait is "grounded" and the shadow

https://doi.org/10.1037/0000391-026
Becoming a Strategic Leader: Capitalize on the Power of Your Personality, by G. W. Watts & L. Blazek

descriptor "judgmental." We know that people who are high in emotional stability are metrically driven. So naturally, Jordan had been measuring success by his personal achievements and individual statistics, and not necessarily by how well the team performed.

Phil Jackson ultimately helped Michael Jordon become more emotionally mature. This process involved diminishing his shadow of being judgmental. Jackson coached him to focus on leveraging his natural personality strength of being grounded to become a truly great leader. This gave him the positive energy to become a more inspiring and supportive team member. His grounded nature offered the team leadership in emotional toughness, resilience, and composure.

As his shadow of being judgmental receded, the other players gained confidence in their own abilities. They began to understand their strengths and they ways each team member could optimally contribute to the whole. Jackson both capitalized on human talent and drove the transaction cycle to obtain superior results. He orchestrated human potential into a dynamic transactional system.

Ultimately, the team was transformed. Jordan moved from the shadow to the light; the rest is history.

The strength of the team lies within the individual. And the strength of the individual lies within the team.

−Phil Jackson, *Eleven Rings: The Soul of Success*

TEAM BUILDING EXAMPLE

Unless the leader fosters a culture of collaboration and respect among team members, the team is just a group of people coming to work or visible on a computer screen. Building a high-functioning team starts with subordinating individual egos. When that occurs, people are free to acknowledge and leverage the strengths of others, appreciating how each role fits into the big picture.

A team of four high-level male executives worked in different countries around the world. Each had a strong resume and great experience and was highly competent. I was brought in to help solve a problem: They fell short when it came to presenting to prospects and clients as a team. There was little collaboration and coordination of effort. When they presented in front of an audience, they didn't hand the ball off to each other effectively. Everyone was fighting for airtime.

There were two main issues. The first was ego. Even if it wasn't verbalized, each team member felt he had the best perspective on what the prospect or client wanted. Each person considered himself the best presenter. Second, nobody understood the personality strengths of the other team members and how those strengths could be capitalized upon. Making matters worse, they didn't respect each other's individual contribution as much as their own. What they didn't see was that the whole had the potential to be much greater than the sum of its parts.

What they didn't see was that the whole had the potential to be much greater than the sum of its parts.

I facilitated individual and group sessions and presented our strategic transacting model. Through the model, I helped them understand where they individually fit best on the transaction cycle and how they added strategic value to the team. During our team-building retreat, I challenged them to put their egos aside and asked the following questions:

1. What is your brand—your two-word positive descriptor?

2. How does your brand add strategic value to the team? Where does your personality strength best fit on the transaction cycle?

3. What strategic value does the team bring to the prospect or client? How does the team effort help the client complete their transactional cycle more quickly?

Many teams don't have a clear appreciation for the skills and personality strengths of its members and how their individual contributions push the ball forward. In this example, this realization was where the "Aha!" moment occurred. The process of developing a positive dialogue among team members begins to create mutual respect and appreciation. When people objectively recognize what part of the transactional cycle they fill (through their unique background and personality strengths), they better understand how they add strategic value. They can then begin to perceive how to best partner with each other.

Our approach with this team was successful in that it facilitated open, honest communication about individual personality strengths. This communication was the basis for helping the team members gain insight into how they could work more effectively together.

It can be a useful exercise for your team to construct a strategic transacting model analysis and for members to place themselves in the cycle based on their personality strengths. Through this process, talent gaps may become apparent, and you might learn where you need to shore up your team. Or you may see that you're appropriately staffed and that the strengths of your people match their respective roles. This is strategic coaching—facilitating a collaborative process that brings people together to define your team's core competency and optimize talent.

TEAM SUCCESS

People want to contribute to team success through their strengths. The drive to add value to the group dynamic is innate. Each person on your team wants to feel accepted and respected. Use the model to visually show them where they fit in and how their contribution is integral to team success.

A big reason for his success as captain is that he is able to understand each individual on the team.

–Comment on MS Dhoni, World Cup-winning captain, Indian national cricket team

CONCLUSION

Becoming a Strategic Leader: Capitalize on the Power of Your Personality was written to help you identify specifically how your personality strengths add strategic value and understand the distinction between a strategic leader and everybody else. By reading these pages and through deep introspection, we hope you're now more enlightened and confident. You now have science-based language to better define yourself and your strengths as you begin to use your personality in a new, more strategic and impacting way.

Throughout the book, we've stressed that success is not about change. As you become more mature, happier, and fulfilled, shadow energy recedes. You don't change—you grow. The difference between change and growth is more than a mindset: Growth is easier, more intuitive, and a lot more fun.

Thank you for reading *Becoming a Strategic Leader: Capitalize on the Power of Your Personality*. We'll end this journey with our favorite quote about our favorite agreeable person:

Be congruent, be authentic, be your true self.

—Henrik Edberg, summarizing Mahatma Gandhi's teachings

https://doi.org/10.1037/0000391-027
Becoming a Strategic Leader: Capitalize on the Power of Your Personality, by G. W. Watts & L. Blazek

Supportive References

Abhishek, K. (2021, April 12). Work with strengths to enhance organizational happiness index. *Forbes*. https://www.forbes.com/sites/forbeshuman resourcescouncil/2021/04/12/work-with-strengths-to-enhance-organizational-happiness-index/?sh=45aa0e8c1562

Allport, G. W. (1961). *Pattern and growth in personality*. Holt, Reinhart & Winston.

Cialdini, R. B. (2021). *Influence: The psychology of persuasion*. Harper Business.

Costa, P. T., Jr., Terracciano, A., & McCrae, R. R. (2001). Gender differences in personality traits across cultures: Robust and surprising findings. *Journal of Personality and Social Psychology, 81*(2), 322–331. https://doi.org/10.1037/0022-3514.81.2.322

Gladwell, M. (2005). *Blink: The power of thinking without thinking*. Little, Brown and Company.

Goleman, D., Boyatzis, R., McKee, A. (2013). *Primal leadership: Unleashing the power of emotional intelligence*. Harvard Business Review.

Hazy, J. K., & Boyatzis, R. E. (2015, 12 June). Emotional contagion and proto-organizing in human interaction dynamics. *Frontiers in Psychology, 6*. https://doi.org/10.3389/fpsyg.2015.00806

Jung, C. G. (1967). *Collected works of C. G. Jung: Vol. 5. Symbols of transformation* (G. Adler & R. F. C. Hull, Eds. & Trans.). Princeton University Press.

Kahneman, D., & Tversky, A. (Eds.). (2000). *Choices, values, and frames*. Cambridge University Press. https://doi.org/10.1017/CBO9780511803475

London, M., Sessa, V. I., & Shelley, L. A. (2023, January). Developing self-awareness: Learning processes for self- and interpersonal growth. *Annual Review of Organizational Psychology and Organizational Behavior, 10*, 261–288. https://doi.org/10.1146/annurev-orgpsych-120920-044531

Maslow, A. H. (1943). A theory of human motivation. *Psychological Review, 50*(4), 370–396. https://doi.org/10.1037/h0054346

McCrae, R. R., & Costa, P. T. (2005). *Personality in adulthood: A five-factor theory perspective* (2nd ed.). Guilford Press.

Murphy, M. (2018, April 15). Neuroscience explains why you need to write down your goals if you actually want to achieve them. *Forbes*. https://www.forbes.com/sites/markmurphy/2018/04/15/neuroscience-explains-why-you-need-to-write-down-your-goals-if-you-actually-want-to-achieve-them/?sh=29ec02347905

Roberts, L. M., Spreitzer, G., Dutton, J. E., Quinn, R. E., Heaphy, E. D., & Barker, B. (2005, January). How to play to your strengths. *Harvard Business Review*. https://hbr.org/2005/01/how-to-play-to-your-strengths

Watts, G. W. (2012). The power of introspection for executive development. *The Psychologist-Manager Journal, 15*(3), 149–157. https://doi.org/10.1080/10887156.2012.701136

Index

About the Authors

George W. Watts, MS, EdD, is chairman of Top Line Talent and a nationally recognized author, behavioral scientist, and senior executive. His passion is inspiring people to mature their natural personality strengths.

George is a frequent speaker and delivers acclaimed leadership training programs throughout the world. He coaches CEOs on how to build and lead formidable C-suite teams. Thousands of people have experienced his approach and commitment to teaching his powerful principles of professional development.

George started his career as a sales trainer and moved into senior management positions. George has been CEO of a mid-cap publicly traded company and executive vice president of two large global service companies. He believes that leadership is the key factor in companies that thrive over generations. He built his behavioral science consulting practice from the ground up, working with a wide variety of companies, from Fortune 100 corporations to entrepreneurial ventures.

He received his doctoral degree in counseling psychology from the College of William and Mary. He is foundation board president for the Society for Psychologists in Leadership. George's book, *Becoming Your Own Business Coach*, is used in graduate school programs. He has also published numerous professional articles on leadership and talent management in both scientific and popular magazines.

Laurie Blazek, BS, MBA, is president and CEO of Top Line Talent and is coauthor of this book and cocreator of the online Top Line Talent leadership development program. Her passion is to help people specifically define who they are when they're at their best.

Laurie has over 25 years of business development, marketing, and leadership experience at large multinational banks, including J. P. Morgan, Citigroup, and Bank of America. She has held senior positions in a wide variety of financial services sectors, including asset-backed finance, corporate and investment banking, leveraged finance, private banking, and financial advising. Her expertise is in developing deep client relationships and organically growing revenue.

Laurie has travelled globally to deliver acclaimed leadership development programs. She currently coaches high-potential professionals and works with them to develop unique and inspiring personal branding statements.

Laurie received an MBA with a concentration in finance from DePaul University. She holds the Certified Financial Planner designation. She is a frequent writer and speaker on a variety of leadership topics. She has also authored numerous professional articles.